John Kehoe

MONEY
success
&you

Published by Zoetic Inc.
P.O. Box 48808
Suite 513 Bentall Centre
Vancouver, British Columbia
V7X 1A6, Canada

Canadian Cataloguing-in-Publication Data

Kehoe, John
   Money, success & you

ISBN 0-9697551-5-5

   1. Success in business. 2. Achievement motivation.
3. Success—Psychological aspects. I. Title. II. Title:
Money, success and you.

HF5386.K44 1998   650.1   C98-900129-6

Cover design by Jim Emerson
Page layout by the Vancouver Desktop Publishing Centre
Printed in Canada by Transcontinental Printing Inc.

Acknowledgments

To Soraya Othman, my business manager and friend, who after fifteen years is going on to new challenges and adventures. Thanks for the good times. I wish you success, and may our friendship continue forever.

To Ric and Jennifer Beairsto for their editing and help; to my wife, Sylvia, for her love and support; and to the countless others who have helped me with this project.

Thanks everybody.

Contents

It All Starts with You

This book is about money and success but, most importantly, it is about you.

Throughout these pages, you will see how financial achievement and self-development can and should go hand in hand. Indeed, when the matter is closely scrutinized, it is evident that the skills needed to become rich and successful are the same skills used to develop character, ability and awareness. Thus, if properly orchestrated, our economic success becomes the means by which we become a better and more fulfilled human being.

The method by which we can accomplish all this in ourselves is the art of self-mastery.

Self-mastery is nothing mysterious. It means looking to see what one's capabilities might be, and then carefully orchestrating and developing those capabilities. It is the ability to know and understand yourself at the deepest level, and to make the changes, both internal and external, that are necessary for your growth and success.

Self-mastery operates on the premise that with training we can grow, and often grow dramatically. That the choices we make in the present eventually determine what happens to us in the future. That when we commit ourselves to excellence, and we do whatever is necessary to bring out the best in ourselves, remarkable changes take place.

Participating in our own evolution in this way becomes both rewarding and exhilarating. For, in developing our talents, we will at the same time discover ourselves at an intimate and deeper level. We will awaken what the German writer Goethe called "the genius, power and magic" in ourselves. This is what's so exciting—that we have the ability to do all this, that whether we proceed is our choice and our choice alone.

This book contains everything you need to know to follow this path. Each chapter contains principles to be mastered. Some will seem strange and unfamiliar; others will be startlingly simple. Embrace each of them and endeavor to perfect them in your life. For it is in the daily application of these principles that the alchemy takes place. This book is to be lived, not just read.

Welcome to the adventure.

PART I

♦ ♦ ♦

THE MIND

What You See
Is What You Get

*It's a funny thing about life, if you refuse to
accept anything but the best, you very often
get it.* —SOMERSET MAUGHAM

How do you perceive the world around you? Is it
friendly? Hostile? Are there many pleasant experiences awaiting you, or is your world mostly onerous,
filled with bitter disappointments? Are there lots of opportunities to get ahead financially, or have most of the good ideas come
and gone? Is life enjoyable, pleasant, boring, exciting, harsh?
How do you see the world you live in?

Each of us will answer these questions in a slightly different
way. We will answer according to our unique personal experience. Sometimes we will contradict each other yet, amazingly
enough, each of us will be right. Whatever you believe is right.
Two totally contradictory beliefs can both be true. But how can
this be? Shouldn't one be true and the other false, or at least
one more true than the other? Well, not necessarily. And to
understand this paradox requires that we look at the nature of
reality in a totally different way, that we discover the truth
behind appearances.

You are a creative law unto yourself, and what you believe
within will be both the lens through which you view the world,
and the attracting force by which countless experiences are

11

drawn to you. Life is much more mysterious than we ever suspected. It is fluid and dynamic in ways we could never imagine. It is literally as diverse and varied as the people who experience it, and what you will discover is that all experience has its root cause within.

HOW WE SEE THE WORLD

We naturally assume that we see our life as it actually is, that we are objective. But this is not the case. We see the world not as it is, but as *we* are. We see it through the lens of our experiences, expectations and beliefs. Our mind processes all our experiences through this filter, and these experiences often get misinterpreted in the process. Discovering what is really going on in our life is far trickier than you might suppose. In fact it is almost impossible, for we do not get to view the world without a lens (a perspective colored by beliefs, expectations and past experiences). The best we can do is to be open to trying different lenses (viewpoints, beliefs), thereby deciding which is more accurate or beneficial for us. It is much the same as going for an eye exam to discover the right lens to counteract an eye deficiency.

If, for example, you find your seeing is hampered, with objects and people seemingly out of focus, you don't say life is out of focus, you don't blame the world out there. You attempt to correct your vision. You try out different lenses—some make your vision seem better, some make it seem worse—and eventually you settle on one that seems right.

Exactly the same with our life. The problems and obstacles we encounter in life are not caused by what is without but by what is within. Your lens is creating your reality. When you change your lens, your reality will change.

HERE'S WHAT HAPPENS

All physical reality is made up of vibrations of energy. The chair you sit on, the walls that surround you, your physical body, everything is made up of vibrations of energy. Our thoughts are also vibrations of energy consisting of the exact same substance. Thoughts that are repeated with feeling and emotion gradually make an imprint on the subconscious. Once this happens our thoughts crystallize into beliefs and begin to vibrate within us, attracting from the outer web of reality the people, circumstances and events that match what is within. I explain this in greater detail in my first book, *Mind Power Into the 21st Century*. I suggest you read both books to fully understand how your mind creates your reality. At this point, however, it is enough to understand that your thoughts are real forces.

You have far more power to create and influence your life than you may be aware of. In fact, you are creating your life this very moment by the thoughts you are choosing to entertain. Your thoughts and beliefs are not merely inner perceptions and attitudes, but are physical vibrations of energy as real as the floor below you. They are the main creative forces in formulating your life and in determining what will happen in your future. Simply stated, your thoughts are the single most important factor in your life, and one over which you have total control. Yet most of us pay them minimal if any attention.

A NEW LEVEL OF THINKING

Looking at life with this new perspective, we can begin to recognize how both the problems and opportunities we meet in life have a direct relationship to our thinking. We see that to try to change the outside world—working harder, changing jobs, moving to another city, blaming other people, coming up with new ideas—will prove fruitless, or at least temporary, until we change the within.

If your core beliefs are that life is difficult, that you'll never get ahead, that there are very few if any opportunities, do you really think working harder, changing cities or jobs will bring you a new level of satisfaction? How could they?

To further illustrate the power of beliefs, let's examine two individuals who hold completely opposite views. One person sees the world as filled with opportunities waiting to be discovered. He imagines himself seizing these opportunities. He believes his actions, creativity and ingenuity will be rewarded abundantly, and that he has what it takes to be tremendously successful. His thoughts, decisions and actions reflect these beliefs.

These beliefs become the lens through which he sees his world. The events of his life, whatever they are, will be interpreted in this way. All available data coming to him will be sifted, weighed and brought to his attention via this lens. These beliefs not only affect his perceptions but also become an inner vibration which, acting upon the outer web of reality, attract, like an unseen magnet, people, circumstances and events to him. These beliefs have a powerful effect in determining what is going to happen to him.

The second individual believes that the odds are stacked against him. He believes that all the good opportunities to make money have been taken, and that those that haven't are too difficult to find. He believes that life is hard and filled with disappointment, and no matter what he does he is probably doomed to failure.

Like the first person, these beliefs become the lens through which he sees the world, and the events of his life will be interpreted in this way. He will weigh and sift through the data of his life using his beliefs as a lens. Information or events running counter to his preconceptions will be ignored to a large degree, or distorted in such a fashion that they will then fit in with what his mind believes is reality. His beliefs also become an inner vibration acting upon the outer web of reality, attracting or repelling people, circumstances and events.

It is not hard to imagine what probable futures exist for each individual. I say probable because anything can happen. But who do you think has a better chance at being successful?

Paradoxically, both individuals are correct in believing what they do. No one truth is more real than the other. You might expect that I would say that the more positive one was closer to reality. Not at all. Both realities are valid and real. And here, before we continue, we need to recognize an important truth. There are numerous diverse realities available to each of us. Each of us will attract according to our beliefs. Each person will reap what he or she sows.

Once we become aware of how much our daily experiences are influenced by these inner programs, it then becomes imperative to examine our beliefs and be prepared to change those beliefs that are limiting us. To do this we need to see and understand the "lens" through which we are viewing the world. To view it without criticism or judgment, and thus to know ourselves at a deep level. This means being courageous, but if we can do so we may discover within ourselves limiting and self-defeating beliefs that are holding us back from achieving what we want.

Each belief must be examined carefully. Not as to whether it's true or not, for our "truth" will always match the lens we wear and thus be validated, but as to what effect it may be having upon our life. Many limiting beliefs have probably been accepted by us, have taken root within the subconscious, and are now reflecting back to us as experience.

Remember all beliefs will seem real in terms of physical data, since your experience in the outside world is the manifestation of these beliefs. So your approach in changing beliefs is not to ask whether they are "real" or not, but rather to ask if these beliefs serve you well. Do these beliefs assist or hinder me in my goals?

I would like you now to list below ten beliefs you hold about money. Do not concern yourself with whether these beliefs are positive or negative, or whether other people believe as you do. We are looking for *your* beliefs. Nobody else need see this list or even know about it. But to be effective it must be done with complete honesty, and from your inner truth and experience. When you're ready, list your beliefs before you continue reading.

1. _____

2. _____

3. _____

4. _____

5. _____

6. _____

7. _____

8. _____

9. _____

10. _____

Now read over the list. Imagine, one by one, these beliefs resonating within you, attracting or repelling circumstances according to their vibration. As you do this, it will be clear to you that some beliefs are working for you and some against you. Now beside those that are working against you, hindering you, place an X.

Now examine each belief with an X independently. Realize that because you believe it and experience it does not mean this belief is real in any absolute sense. It may be real for you in your life and experience, but what does that prove? Only that you are experiencing that reality. But is this belief and truth real for everyone? Here we can test this belief. Ask yourself these questions:

◆ Does every single person have this belief?
◆ Does it conform to every lens?
◆ Are there people who do not have this belief, and if so what are their experiences?

By examining beliefs in this way what you will find is that no belief or truth is absolute in any real sense. This being so, you can choose to free yourself of any undesirable belief and take on whatever new one you want. You literally get to choose your beliefs.

Changing beliefs can be accomplished if you're willing to keep an open mind. It will take discipline, and initially what you will be doing will defy your logic and senses, but this is a small price to pay for harnessing the powers of your mind and taking charge of your destiny.

Before we leave this chapter let me state clearly that no one can change your beliefs for you, nor can they be forced upon you from without. You and only you can decide what it is you will choose to believe.

Let me also say that the system I'm proposing to you cannot be explored half-heartedly, but will demand a genuine commitment. I am not offering a philosophy but a practice, and this practice will take effort. Somewhere between five to twenty minutes a day is necessary. Are you up for the challenge and adventure?

I hope so, because the astounding fact is that you can create whatever reality you choose by working with your thoughts and beliefs. Once you begin applying these methods this fact will become self-evident, and will be validated by the new realities you will be manifesting. A glorious life of power, abundance, health and prosperity awaits you. It all lies within.

Changing Beliefs

One of the greatest discoveries a man makes,
one of his greatest surprises, is to find he can
do what he was afraid he couldn't do.

—HENRY FORD

Beliefs are as necessary to us as our physical organs. We cannot exist without them. We need them as parameters to interpret what is happening in our life. One could never be without beliefs, nor would you want to be. What you do want, however, is to consciously decide the beliefs you want working for you. To choose the lens you will view the world through. And here your choices are unlimited.

You are not at the mercy of your past experiences, unless you believe that you are. With this new system you are free to break away from any past conditioning or limited circumstances by simply changing your thoughts and beliefs. When you change these you change everything. The future that you will encounter in your life is not preordained, nor does it happen arbitrarily. As you have seen in the previous chapter, your reality is forever being moulded and created from your thoughts and beliefs. Your possible future—and there are literally thousands of possible futures—is being formed by what you think and believe today. The present is the womb by which the future will be born. The future is dynamically alive within you now. You hold within you your own destiny. Change your thoughts and beliefs and you will change your future.

Once you fully recognize the power and influence beliefs have in your life, the next step becomes obvious. Change the beliefs that are limiting and holding you back, and create powerful new beliefs that serve and uplift you, beliefs that will take you wherever you wish to go.

There are three main methods for doing this, and all three should be employed. You can begin by using them individually or in combination with each other. Either way, you will eventually be working with all three.

1. Repattern Your Past

Don't spend time and energy looking back at your life to find out why you have a certain limiting belief. Why bother? To look backward in this way will only lead you into the habit of seeking negative examples that verify your old belief. Your past has been distorted by the lens you have chosen to examine it through. What is accomplished by searching the past with the same old lens, other than to further reinforce that limiting belief already held within you? This is why much psychotherapy proves futile, simply miring the patient further in his or her own muck.

A great many of the unsatisfactory conditions in our life have resulted from our becoming frightened or confused during an unpleasant experience. We began to doubt ourselves, and started concentrating upon negative aspects of our lives, thereby eventually creating that imprint within us.

For example, one person, because of an unpleasant experience, begins to doubt his ability to get along with others. So he searches his past with an "I don't relate well with people" lens, and much to his horror finds many experiences to support this idea. His mind begins to feed on these memories. His remembering becomes highly selective. Without even realizing it, he invents his own history, and furthermore convinces himself that this history represents an accurate picture of who he is. However, if this person had journeyed through his memories with the lens, "I get along great with people," trying to find a different kind of proof, he would undoubtedly have discovered many instances when he got on very well with others. However you choose to view your life, through whatever lens you have constructed, this will structure and filter your memories, and you will always be able to justify your belief with "proof."

So in changing beliefs you must practice changing your lens. Look through your past in a new way, looking for new, forgotten or ignored truths. If you lack confidence, for example, search your past for instances when you were confident. If you are honest in this search you will find lots of examples of you performing tasks assuredly. But you must search with the lens, "I'm confident," not the "I lack confidence" lens. Each lens will produce a different set of examples. There will be numerous examples of both. It all depends upon which you want to emphasize.

In almost all cases of present limitation you have programmed yourself to stress negative aspects relating to that part of your life. We all do it. So to rid yourself of these restrictions, you repattern your past from the present. Whatever your circumstances, use the past as a rich source of power, looking through it for long ignored successes. Restructure your past. Reinvent it. Rediscover it. It's like finding a bank account with money that you didn't know you possessed. Whatever you want to become or create in your current life, you can find ample evidence of it already happening to you in the past if you will only change your lens.

THE PRESENT IS YOUR POINT OF POWER

Stop for a moment and realize that the present is your point of power. When you are thinking about the past or imagining the future, both these actions happen in the present. When you act upon your life, it takes place in the present. In fact nothing you can do will ever happen outside of the present. So choosing in the present to reframe your past and future is incredibly powerful.

An example: Pick a positive quality about yourself that you are proud of and absolutely certain you possess. Perhaps that you are caring, loving and compassionate towards others. Now, using your memory, search your past for times when you were not caring, times when you were selfish, mean, unkind and hurtful. Locate a number of these examples. Now imagine yourself lingering on these images each day. Each day you purposely recall these images and feel bad about them. Soon you begin telling yourself that you are indeed mean-spirited and selfish.

If you continued this practice you would literally hypnotize yourself into believing that this selfish, mean-spirited person is who you are, and then you would begin to become this person. This belief would become self-fulfilling.

Likewise with our negative qualities. We have programmed ourselves without even realizing what we've been doing. We have hypnotized ourselves through repetition and selective memory into believing that this reduced version of ourselves is who we are. But you can change this. You can look within yourself for evidence of whatever positive qualities you desire. Examine your past with this in mind. Do not let the past reinforce your limitations; use it to reinforce what you wish to become. Be diligent about this. Use the selective process of your mind to your advantage.

2. Imprinting

What is 6 x 6?, 7 x 5?, 9 x 9? How is it that you know these answers instantly, quicker than you can punch the numbers into a calculator? It is because you have imprinted the multiplication tables into your consciousness. Think back to when you were in school. Think of how many times these tables were repeated, written out and practiced, until eventually they became imprinted into your consciousness. And now they are firmly imprinted. You need not practice them or refresh yourself—they are there for life.

What you have done with the multiplication tables can also be done with new beliefs you wish to permanently imprint into your consciousness. The process is exactly the same, and the repetition equally important.

For five or ten minutes a day concentrate your attention as vividly as possible upon one simple statement. For example, if you wanted to imprint a belief about your subconscious that would help you to be successful you might use this one: "My subconscious mind is my partner in success." Having picked the statement you wish to use, begin to concentrate on it. Try to feel the statement in whatever way possible. Do not allow your mind to drift to other subjects. If it does, bring your attention back to your statement and refocus. Feel the power and implication of what you are saying. Let it become alive within you. Repeat it over and over, allowing your mind to absorb its message. If your mind insists on images, channel the images toward your declaration. Close yourself off to all other truths or realities, focusing solely upon the feeling and power of the statement.

The repetition, whether verbal or mental, is important because it activates neurological patterns. Do not strain. Do not question or doubt. Enjoy the process. Claim it absolutely within. Lose yourself as completely as you can in this one statement. Let it vibrate within you, letting you and it become one. Feel its power. Let it energize you.

When the exercise is finished, do not dwell upon it, second guess yourself, wonder if it's true. Put if from your mind until the next day, when you will repeat the process. Realize you are using the present as a moment of power to insert new beliefs that will naturally be materialized. It will happen automatically.

You may want to experiment with the precise wording of your statement. Often it takes three or four revisions before the statement feels exactly right. Once you have it right then simply continue with it. You may experience spectacular results almost immediately. If you do, wonderful, but do not let this fool you into discontinuing the exercise. Often when people begin this process they do not realize how quickly results can be seen, and they become overexcited about the results achieved. In their excitement they forget to continue the exercise. If you want permanent results, you must fully imprint the new belief. A minimum of sixty to ninety days is necessary for a permanent imprint to take hold.

3. Action

The sooner you begin to act upon the new beliefs you are creating, the better. Otherwise you are not trusting and using the present. If you are poor and want to have more money and you're trying to establish a belief in abundance while still faced with your lack, then begin demonstrating abundance. In your outer reality take some symbolic action that shows you are changing. Maybe give some money (no matter how little) to charity. Indulge yourself somehow. A nice meal, a new article of clothing, a little gift to yourself.

Or if you're lacking confidence, you would first repattern your past, searching and finding past examples of you being confident and you would focus daily on these. You would also imprint new empowering beliefs supporting your confidence, and then finally you act as if it were true. Bring action into the formula. No matter how small or inconsequential the action may seem, it is a huge step. It is a manifestation in outer reality.

Responding to your new beliefs in this way is sending a strong signal to your subconscious that new realities are beginning to take hold, that you are willing to change, that you are cooperating with the process, that it is in fact already happening.

The initiative must come from you. Challenge yourself to find ways to demonstrate your changing reality.

Desire

*First you fuel the desire, then the desire will
fuel you.* —NAPOLEON HILL

Knowing what one wants in life is not enough. Nor will
wishing or hoping to achieve success help you. You must
go one step further and add the vibration of desire to
the mix. It is desire that acts as the catalyst with your thoughts
and beliefs, supplying the needed emotion that the subconscious mind requires in order to translate your thoughts into
reality.

All the great men and women achievers of the past have
known this. They have all shared this one overwhelming simi-
larity—a burning desire to achieve their objectives.

Thomas Edison experienced more than 10,000 failures
before he perfected the light bulb. His desire to succeed never
waned. Wilbur and Orville Wright suffered through years of
humiliation and ridicule for daring to believe they could make
a vehicle fly through the air. Yet the strength of their purpose
and desire allowed them to persevere until they produced the
first successful airplane. Henry Ford went bankrupt twice
before the first Model T rolled off the assembly line, yet he
never wavered from his determination to mass-produce the
automobile.

Ted Turner also knew what he wanted. It was not a mere wish or hope that he had, but a burning desire to achieve his objective—owning and running a media and communications empire. When this thought first entered his mind, he owned a tiny billboard company in Atlanta. He began to build his dream by purchasing a small radio station, followed by a lackluster UHF (ultra-high-frequency) television station that less than half the TV sets in the area were able to receive. The year was 1968. Right from the beginning he ran into problems. The TV station was hemorrhaging money. By 1970 it was losing over $700,000 a year. "The station will bring down the whole company," said Irwin Mazo, Turner's accountant at the time, who promptly quit.

"It's pretty tough when your own accountant quits because he thinks you're doomed," said Ted. Others at this point might have backed off and been more prudent, heeding their accountant's advice. Or maybe they would have given up, thinking their dream was unattainable. But not Ted Turner. What was his response? He went out and bought another station. His rationale? It was only losing $30,000 a month! And not only did he purchase it; in the process he further assumed nearly $3 million in liabilities.

Now at this point, I would like to say to the reader that a strong desire to achieve your goal might cause a man to act in ways that seem crazy to others. So crazy that even his accountant may quit, and for Turner that was not all. Several of his top people quit as well, certain that Ted was headed for disaster. But they could not see what Ted saw. For in addition to a lightning-quick mind, Turner also possessed a sixth sense that allowed him to see beyond conventional wisdom and act accordingly.

And sure enough, within several years he had turned his struggling Atlanta station into America's first "super station," beaming its programming off a satellite into homes all over

North America. Revenue began pouring in, but rather than stop while he was ahead, Turner set his sights even higher. In 1979 he borrowed over $27 million to finance CNN, an untried "all news station" that many said no one would watch. And in the beginning, it looked like they were right. CNN lost over $70 million in its first five years. During this time, Turner had a sign on his desk that read, "Lead, follow or get out of the way." He knew what he wanted, and nothing was going to stop him. His burning desire overcame all else. And here we come to one of the secrets of desire. A strong desire to have or do what you have set your mind to recognizes no such thing as failure. All disappointments, problems and setbacks are but temporary obstacles on the way to success.

By 1984, CNN had turned the corner and finally began to show a profit. Then in 1987 Turner made his biggest gamble to date. With a combination of junk bonds and other financing that highly leveraged his company, he bought MGM Studios for a whopping $1.2 billion. It saddled him with almost a billion dollars in debt. Most analysts at the time thought Turner had overpaid MGM's former owners by at least $300 million. One Hollywood veteran was quoted in *Fortune* magazine as saying, "Turner got the worst screwing in the history of American business." But they did not know what Ted Turner knew. Nor could they see the profit he would one day derive from the MGM film library of over 3,000 titles, how he would repackage this content and broadcast it on still more TV stations. His desire to have his media empire, and his sixth sense drawing upon the wisdom of his subconscious, let Ted see what no one else could. With boldness, some called it reckless boldness, he pursued his goal, never wavering.

"Turner has an uncanny ability to obliterate anything and

everything peripheral to his immediate objective," said Porter Bibb, former White House correspondent for *Newsweek*. "This is why he is so successful."

By 1990, a mere three years later, with the media landscape changing rapidly and the cost of programming skyrocketing, Turner's instincts were again proved right. His company entered into a period of explosive growth and profits. The MGM deal was suddenly called by *Institutional Investor,* "one of the deals of the decade."

In 1997 Turner Broadcasting System merged with Time Warner to become one of the largest communication and media companies in the world. Ted Turner's media empire was now a resounding international success, worth billions of dollars. He had revolutionized the broadcast industry and made Marshall McLuhan's "global village" a reality. He had rewritten the very definition of news as something that is happening rather than something that has happened. He had built the largest news gathering organization in the world. He also controlled the largest library of motion pictures anywhere, and one of the largest collections of animated films. His broadcasts reached over 120 countries.

In the merger, and for his efforts, Turner personally received over $3 billion in cash and stock. He had achieved his wildest dreams.

The same force of desire and determination that Ted Turner harnessed is available to each and every one of us. Follow these four steps and watch desire come alive within you:

Step 1
Write down a clear and concise statement of what it is you wish to obtain.

Step 2

Outline what you intend to do or give to achieve this objective. There is no such thing as something for nothing. What skills, knowledge, disciplines and actions will you obtain or practice? Be clear and concise.

Step 3

Promise yourself to let nothing stop you from obtaining your objectives. Make a commitment to yourself to do whatever is necessary to achieve your goal. Be firm in your resolution.

Step 4

Read this statement over twice every day. Read it upon rising in the morning, and again before you go to sleep, and begin immediately to put this plan to work. When reading your statement, magnetize your mind to the reality of achieving your goal. See and feel yourself already in possession of that which you desire. As days turn into weeks and then months, this ritual will be the source of a great amount of power and inspiration for you.

A strong, burning desire to obtain and possess the goal you are pursuing is the starting point for all achievement. This isn't a vague wish or a simple hope; it is something much more powerful than that. Burning desire, when properly ignited, takes on a life and power of its own and empowers you in hundreds of different ways.

There is a Zen parable that will help to illustrate what I mean. A Zen monk and his student were walking by the river when the young student begins to plead with his master, "How do I become enlightened? What must I do?" The master grabbed him roughly, pulled him into the river and pushed him under the water until the young student was completely submerged.

The Zen master continued to hold the student under water and soon the student began to thrash frantically. But still the master held him under the water. Desperately the student tried to free himself, to no avail. Finally, just at the point of drowning, the master released his grip and the student surfaced, gasping for air.

"What were you thinking while I held you under the water?" the master asked. "At first I thought of many things," the student answered. "But after a few seconds, when there was no sign that you would let me up, all I could think of was: Air! Air! Give me air!"

"When you desire enlightenment with the same intensity," said the master smiling, "you will soon have it."

The same applies to achieving your goals. You must desire it with your whole being. Desire is the fuel that propels you towards your objectives and influences your thoughts and actions. Desire helps you overcome obstacles and draw inspiration from your subconscious. A strong desire combined with prosperity beliefs and continuous action towards your goal will attract to you the people, circumstances and situations you need to be successful.

Prosperity Consciousness

To them that hath . . . more shall be given. To
them that hath not, even what little they have
will be taken away. —LUKE 19:26

I f you wish to attract success and abundance into your life
you must program your subconscious mind with prosperity
beliefs. These beliefs, once internalized, become an incredibly powerful attracting force to bring to you the people,
circumstances and opportunities needed for your success.
Prosperity beliefs produce within an individual a prosperity
consciousness.

Scarcity beliefs create a scarcity consciousness, and scarcity
consciousness consists of a number of limiting beliefs. Scarcity
consciousness vibrates with fear, lack, failure and disappointment. It expects the worst and that is what it attracts.

One cannot possess both a prosperity and scarcity consciousness at the same time. They do not and cannot inhabit the same
mind. One or the other will be dominant. Nor can you switch
day by day. This is not a suit of clothes that one puts on and off
at will. Either consciousness will be fairly well entrenched with
beliefs, and although it can be changed, it takes both awareness
and commitment to do so.

While it is obvious that a prosperity consciousness is more
desirable and advantageous, it does not happen by chance. You

must create prosperity beliefs within yourself. Let me be very blunt: Until you start reprogramming your subconscious mind and thereby become committed and emotionally involved in your own prosperity, you are unlikely to succeed. This is why so many do not succeed in their life. They want to be successful but have not created the necessary consciousness to attract success. Success does not happen by magic, nor does it happen by hard work alone. You may work as hard as you choose, but if you possess scarcity consciousness you will be sabotaged and frustrated every step of the way.

There are many prosperity beliefs one can internalize. The following four will give you a starting point and, once adopted and internalized, they will act as a foundation whereby others can be added at will. Imprint these four beliefs using the techniques explained previously and enjoy what happens as they begin vibrating within you, attracting the people, circumstances and events that harmonize with the prosperity consciousness you have created.

PROSPERITY BELIEF 1
Opportunities are everywhere.

There are a staggering number of opportunities to be successful and make a great deal of money. Our dynamic, ever-changing marketplace is bursting with new and exciting opportunities simply awaiting the shrewd individual who can discover them. Many are perfectly suited to your particular skills and talents. However, you are unlikely to discover them until you begin vibrating with this belief.

Read the upcoming chapter entitled Opportunities are Everywhere and you will begin to understand where your opportunities may exist.

PROSPERITY BELIEF 2
Success and abundance is the natural law of the universe.

Success and abundance exist everywhere in nature. The eagle was created to soar high above the trees, and it does so with graceful ease. No one who has ever witnessed an eagle in flight fails to be moved by its beauty and power. The eagle's eyes are uniquely designed to locate small prey and fish at over a thousand feet, and they do so very well. The eagle is a successful creation of nature, with features specifically designed for its unique purpose.

Trees successfully grow from small seeds into towering giants. Flowers successfully bloom in the springtime. The sun's rays successfully travel from the ball of fire 93 million miles away and nourish each plant, flower and tree on the planet, and these plants in turn successfully transform this energy through the miraculous process of photosynthesis.

Our body successfully assimilates the food we eat and discards the rest as waste. Snow falls in the mountains, melts in spring, runs down streams and rivers to the ocean, eventually evaporating and successfully continuing the cycle, once again falling somewhere as precipitation. Planet earth successfully orbits the sun every 365 days, and our universe is successfully unfolding in its own diverse, unique and mysterious way.

Success is the natural law of the universe. Abundance too.

Abundance is all around you if you will stop to notice it. Count the blades of grass on your lawn—you cannot because they exist in such abundance. Try to count the stars in the sky—you cannot because they exist in such abundance. Walk through a forest; count the trees, again incredible abundance.

Nature is extravagant, lavish and plentiful. Success and

abundance are the natural way of things—the way the universe naturally unfolds.

And yet in the affairs of men and women we see both poverty and abundance. Some people are tremendously successful while others are not. Why is this? If success and abundance exist so effortlessly and lavishly within nature, why not within human-kind, for are we not also part of this grand scheme?

Perhaps the answer lies in how we use our consciousness. Could it be that somewhere along the line we fell out of rhythm with the greater scheme of things? And if so how do we realign ourselves? Upon reflection, one sees that if abundance and success are the natural conditions of life, then by bringing ourselves into harmony with them we too will experience these conditions. Attune your consciousness to the truth and beauty of success and abundance; imprint them within and recognize success and abundance whenever and wherever they appear.

Align yourself with all that is true and noble and in harmony with the greatest good.

Success and abundance are the natural laws of the universe, and each of us has the responsibility to behold this truth and manifest it in our lives. Only then can our gifts of creativity and productivity be shared with the world.

When we bring forth our talents and manifest success in our calling, whether we are a chef, a salesperson, a food manager, a schoolteacher or an entrepreneur, others are blessed and receive the benefit. And this is one of the truths of success. Our success helps many people. Our failure helps no one. This is why success is imprinted into all creatures large and small, into all life forms, whether plants or animals. Success is necessary to all things and everything is wired to achieve this success. Yes, there is failure too, but failure is the exception. It is a collapse of the system, an abnormality.

We as human beings also contain within us the neuro-electrical circuits to succeed. We too are wired for success. All that is required is for us to awaken to the truth of our potential and activate the programs, to actively participate as programmer of our consciousness.

PROSPERITY BELIEF 3
I have the talent and capabilities to be tremendously successful.

No one will ever be successful until they believe that they have the talents and capabilities to be successful, that life affords them the opportunities to express this talent and be richly compensated. You must believe this absolutely. Not hope it is true, or wish it were, but truly believe it with all your heart and soul. Do you believe this? Answer honestly, do you?

If you do believe this, great. It is one of the cornerstones of a prosperity consciousness. With this belief you are well on your way. If you don't, do not despair. You have only to awaken to the remarkable truth of your potential and begin applying the principles of this book. Very soon you too will come to believe in your ability to succeed. After all you have been successfully wired for success. All that is necessary is for you to choose and activate the required programs.

The principle of unlimited potential within each of us is a very exciting idea. The notion that we can grow and change and develop whatever talents we need is indeed exhilarating. Each of us possesses free will—we have the freedom to choose our thoughts, beliefs and actions. We can pursue any interest in whatever area we desire. We literally can do or become whatever we want. We are not limited in any way, so long as our thoughts are not limited.

PROSPERITY BELIEF 4
My subconscious mind is my partner in success.

As incredible as it might seem, your subconscious contains within it the entire web of all reality. It has access to all experiences, all knowledge; there is nothing it does not know. It does not have the boundaries, limitations and restrictions of our conscious mind.

Your subconscious mind acts independently of your five senses and personal reality, and when properly directed it will bring you insights, plans and ideas on any area of your life where you need guidance. It will further warn you of impending dangers in time to avoid them, and reveal to you everything you need to know to be successful. It is a treasure house of wisdom, knowledge and inspiration that you can access time and time again.

It is also within the subconscious that one of the most astounding transformations in nature takes place. It is here where thoughts and beliefs, when mixed with emotion begin to translate themselves into physical reality. We hold within us this power. This knowledge of the interaction of your conscious and subconscious minds will enable you to transform your life.

Sadly, too often the subconscious is understood only intellectually, as a concept. If you wish to use it effectively, you will want to have a greater understanding and realization of what it is and how it works. This can only be achieved by repeatedly reminding yourself of the existence of the subconscious, its power and potential. If you do, gradually it will dawn on you that you do indeed possess this power, and then you will begin to use it with excitement and enthusiasm.

The subconscious mind functions constantly, day and night, whether you make any effort to influence it or not. Your subconscious cannot and will not remain idle. If you fail to consciously attend to it, it will feed upon the thoughts that reach it as the result of your neglect, and here is the cause of so much failure. The subconscious does not reason things out like your conscious mind, and it does not argue with you or reject anything as undesirable. Your subconscious mind accepts whatever is impressed upon it. It is amenable to suggestion and will work with any images or beliefs. Negative, limiting beliefs will work in your subconscious mind and will attract the corresponding experiences to you just as effectively as will positive beliefs.

Positive and negative emotions cannot occupy the mind at the same time. One or the other must dominate. It is your responsibility to make sure that positive beliefs constitute the dominating influence of your mind. Here the law of habit will come to your aid. Form the habit of daily imprinting prosperity beliefs. Soon prosperity consciousness will so dominate your mind that negatives cannot enter.

Do not become discouraged if you cannot do this upon the first attempt. Remember that the subconscious mind may be voluntarily directed only through habit. Be patient. Be persistent.

Your subconscious mind is indeed your partner in success, but it is a partner with whom you must work in harmony. It will follow your lead only after you have taken the initiative. You must first imprint upon it what you want it to do. You must take the first steps. You cannot be vague. You must be very specific. You must work diligently and persistently with your thoughts and beliefs. That is what the subconscious mind needs. It needs you to create the blueprint. Otherwise it will create from a myriad of contradictory and limiting beliefs and your experiences in life will mirror this process.

Once you have accepted the existence of the subconscious mind as a reality, and understand its possibilities as a medium for translating your desires into their physical or monetary equivalent, you will comprehend the full significance of creating a prosperity consciousness. You will then have no difficulty in finding the time to daily imprint these new and empowering beliefs.

I SEEM TO BE A VERB

"I seem to be a verb." I was sitting in the audience a number of years ago with about a thousand other people when Buckminster Fuller, the brilliant futurist and inventor, uttered these words. They hit me like an arrow. It was as if he was speaking just to me. "I am a becoming. I am action. I am a process," he continued. His theory, so eloquently presented, is that each of us is "a perpetual happening," and it had a profound impact on me. He gave me courage and insight. He taught me that our decisions and actions impact our life and the lives of others immensely, and that this process is happening continuously. We persist in thinking of ourselves as nouns, things, locked into who we are, when in fact the exact opposite is true. We are forever evolving, changing, becoming, and we can use this process to our great advantage by embracing change as our greatest ally.

Direct yourself towards what you want to become and leave behind all that no longer serves you. If you have a weakness—change it. Lack of confidence or initiative—change it. You are forever becoming—all change exists as a potential within you. Thoughts of confidence will draw confidence from the reservoir within you. Likewise thoughts of courage and action will set your life in motion toward positive change. How you envision yourself is what you will become. When you change, everything changes. When you change, the world is turned upside down and inside out. It's that dramatic. A new life is but a new mind. Awaken now, this very moment, to your potential. See your life as it is and how you want it to be. See the actions, choices and beliefs necessary to take you there. Are you ready to go? Would you like to begin the journey now? You are the programmer—write and activate the program.

Is Rich a Four-Letter Word?

It's not that I like money so much, it's just that I find it soothes my nerves. —JOE LOUIS

Every year I conduct a number of seminars worldwide, teaching individuals the principles of money and success. In doing this, I've discovered a very interesting phenomenon: *A lot of people are afraid to be rich*. One part of them wants to be rich of course, but another part of them feels it's wrong, or that they will have to give up too much to become rich. I keep hearing people say such things as: "I'll have to work too hard for it," or "I'll have to cheat and go against my values," or "Money can't buy happiness," or "People with money are greedy," or "If I have a lot others will be going without," or "I'll have to neglect my family." And a host of similar comments.

If you believe that you'll neglect your family, become greedy, lose your friends or have to give up too much to become rich, then no matter how much you think you want it, there will always be this other part of you that will fight the possibility every step of the way.

Even one of the above beliefs deeply ingrained within your subconscious is enough to sabotage your efforts at creating wealth. If you related to any of the above beliefs, what you need is a set of new beliefs, a new model of success to inflame your imagination, a model which includes your deepest values and sees your attainment of money and success as a part of the greater good of humanity. Let's examine some of the limiting beliefs people often mistakenly take upon themselves. I'll respond to each one as we go.

1. Money can't buy happiness.

Response: No, but then neither can poverty. Happiness comes from within. It comes from understanding yourself and building a life that has value and meaning. You can do this with or without money.

2. People with money are greedy.

Response: Some of them are. So are some middle-class people, and some poor people as well. Some people with money are incredibly generous and compassionate—it's not the money but the person. You will find both greedy and generous people at all economic levels.

3. I will have to work too hard. I'll neglect my family. I'll have to give up too much. (There are a number of beliefs centered upon this theme.)

Response: Some people will indeed give up too much and neglect their families in their pursuit of success, and this is unfortunate. It's also totally unnecessary. It shows that they're out of balance and have adopted the faulty belief, "The harder I work the more successful I'll be." But because some will do it this way, does that mean this is the only way to be successful? What about those who do it while raising and nourishing their families with love and attention? What about those who do it on their own terms and in their own ways, combining fun, leisure and passion. There are tens of thousands who have done it this way. I have done it this way. In no way did I compromise my values or lifestyle in gaining the wealth I have. It's not necessary.

And let us not overlook how many families will suffer because there is not enough money. Families with two parents working long hours just to get by. How many people give up too much of their lives struggling at jobs they dislike? Is it money or the lack of money that is the root of these problems?

4. Money is unspiritual.

Response: This comes from the biblical quotation, "The love of money is the root of all evil." The love of money to the exclusion of all else perhaps. The love of money without understanding how to use it to benefit yourself and others perhaps. But money is a form of energy that has incredible potential for good. If money is so bad in spiritual terms, why did Christ speak so highly of King Solomon? There are a number of passages in the Bible where Solomon is spoken of in terms of the highest esteem. Who was King Solomon?—the richest man in the world at the time. So obviously riches by themselves can't be bad. It must be something else.

5. If I have a lot, others will go without.

Response: There are two possible perspectives here. There is the "holographic" model, which says the universe is unlimited in its supply and the more money you create for yourself, the more exists for everyone. Then there is the "limited pie" model, which suggests that there is only so much money to go around, that money is finite and the more you have, the less there is available for others. Ironically both models support the importance of creating large amounts for yourself.

First the holographic model: Each of us is creating and living a life of our own making. Consciousness is unlimited and we can create and manifest according to our understanding of this fact. The money we create in our life adds to the whole and never takes away. There is an unlimited supply of money that can never be exhausted. Notice I'm not saying an unlimited supply of resources, which are obviously finite and must be managed, but rather an unlimited supply of money. Notice for example how much money is made in the service industry, using few if any natural resources. There are hundreds of billions of dollars waiting to be created, and this is only a drop in the bucket of how much money can be manifested. The supply is unlimited.

Now the limited pie model: There is a finite amount of money in the world, says this theory. There is only so much to go around, and if I have a lot, others will have little. Well, let's assume you're a millionaire or you're worth a few hundred million, or even a few billion. Who exactly is going without by your having this money, and if you were to let it be reabsorbed into the economic system, would these people suddenly have more?

If there is a finite amount of money available then all the more reason for you to make lots and then be a good custodian of it. Use it in socially responsible ways. If you have based your desire to have money upon a foundation that recognizes social responsibility, then you will naturally disperse it in ways that will benefit others. Who better to have a lot of money than those of us who will manage and use it well? The potential to do good with money is enormous.

LOVE THE GOOD THAT MONEY CAN DO

Come into a new more empowering awareness of the dynamic creativity and power that money possesses. Let us set aside for a moment the obvious benefits that money affords a person. The freedom, the material comforts, the choices and availability of self-expression, which are all valid and good reasons to have money. Let's go a step further and examine money's potential to transform our world, and why if we're socially responsible it is valuable for us to possess it.

Most if not all of the good works that happen on this planet come from a combination of money and vision.

Mother Theresa died in 1997 and left a legacy of dedicated selflessness. She took a vow of poverty and worked tirelessly all her life to help the poor and homeless. But her foundation did not take a vow of poverty. It actively raised millions of dollars every year to support hospitals and shelters. Without the abundance of money flowing through her foundation, the effect of her work would have been minimal. Money was and continues to be an important part of the equation that allows her work to proceed.

A number of years ago the Costa Rican government was at a crossroads. They were about to sell the last virgin rainforests to the forest industry for $100 million. Environmentalists were up in arms, and rightfully so, but as a government official said at the time, "We are a poor nation and need the money for education and health care." A small group of dedicated people devoted themselves to coming up with a solution that would save the rainforest. Many options were considered and rejected, and then someone came up with the outrageous idea of buying the rainforest and preserving it as a natural park. Great idea, but where do you get $100 million? Most people would dismiss this idea as ludicrous and impossible. Luckily the world is filled with individuals whose desire to accomplish their mission in life recognizes no such word as impossible.

The desire to save the rainforest led several of these people to take this unorthodox approach. It was not easy. Numerous times they were called dreamers, utterly unrealistic. Sometimes they wondered themselves if this was true, but they continued to search for ways to raise the money, rebounding again and again from constant rejection. They approached numerous organizations, all of which turned them down—except one. The World Bank finally agreed to undertake the project and the rainforest was saved. Now it is the pride of the Costa Rican government and a natural treasure to all who visit its pristine beauty. This happened because a few very dedicated people devoted themselves to its outcome. It happened because of vision and persistence. But mostly it happened because $100 million changed hands.

Love the good that money can do. Appreciate and acknowledge the good that money can do. Recognize that your success has the potential to help many people and that your failure will help no one. It is your duty and responsibility to succeed.

NEW ROLE MODELS

We need to study the lives of individuals who have used their success and money to benefit others, who have lived full, exciting lives and been an asset to society. We need to rid ourselves of the outdated and erroneous stereotype of greedy, selfish millionaires thinking only of themselves. Yes, they exist, but so do their counterparts, and it is these individuals who we will model ourselves after as we create our success and abundance.

Let's look at Ted Turner again. I have shared with you his business acumen and ability to gain tremendous wealth. Now let's look at some of the things he does with his money. He is a remarkable role model.

"Organizations have a responsibility," Peter Drucker, author and well-respected business consultant, once said, "to find an approach to basic social problems that can match their competence." Turner Broadcasting System certainly became a prototype of this philosophy. Ted Turner had a passion to help make the world a better place. He was keenly interested in population control, environmental issues, and Native American Indian rights to name but a few causes. He founded the Better World Society, which has as its slogan, "Harnessing the Power of Television to Make a Better World."

"Broadcasting has a responsibility to point certain things out to people," Turner declared, "that's what Better World is trying to do." Between 1985 and 1989 the Better World Society funded over fifty documentaries with limited commercial value but with huge potential to influence and educate. In 1990, with $500,000 in cash prizes, Ted established the Turner Tomorrow Awards, intended to inspire writers and activists around the world to submit their own "positive solutions to global problems." And Turner has supported numerous other groups whose objective is to make the world a better place.

In October 1997 Turner made headlines around the world when he announced that he was giving $1 billion to the United Nations to be used for humanitarian purposes. "I know what money can do," he said. "I want to help. I want to be a role model. We all need to contribute. Those of us that have more need to give more. Those that have less [need to] give less, but we can all contribute."

When I read what Ted had done it reminded me of a statement that author and philosopher Marshall McLuhan once made: "There are no passengers on Spaceship Earth; we are all crew."

Make no mistake; Ted Turner is no Mother Theresa. He certainly has not taken a vow of poverty and enjoys his money to the fullest. That's wonderful, but what is even more exciting is how he consistently uses it for good. And we have not heard the last from Ted. I have a feeling he's only begun. And there are countless others like him. People like George Soros, who uses his wealth to assist the new democracies of Eastern Europe. There are lots of examples of good custodians of money out there. Don't be deceived by believing different.

BUILD YOUR DESIRE FOR MONEY ON A FIRM FOUNDATION OF INTEGRITY AND GOODNESS

If you want to attract money in large amounts you must come to a realization of what money can do. Understand the potential of money to create immense good in the world, not just the enjoyment that you personally will derive from its accumulation. Tie your desire for money to beliefs that encourage you to succeed for this reason. You cannot be timid. You must align your desire for success and money to the highest values, so that you feel inspired to do whatever is necessary to attract these conditions to you.

Muhammad Ali was a master of this. Whenever he fought he was always fighting "for the little people." For the drug addict, the welfare mother, the little boy without a father; he aligned his success with that of the black nation. He was fighting and winning for them. This gave him added determination and inflamed his desire to win to where he refused to accept defeat.

The fact that most of his opponents were also black in no way affected his resolve. In his mind he was doing it for his people, and this helped him immeasurably.

I used this same technique on my way to first becoming a millionaire. When I began teaching the powers of the mind, I insisted that I demonstrate these powers in my life. I didn't feel I had the authority to be on stage, sharing these truths, unless I could unequivocally demonstrate them. At the time I was virtually broke. I therefore demanded of myself that I demonstrate abundance by becoming a millionaire. I've only had two financial goals in my life. One was to become a millionaire, and that I achieved. The second was to earn $1 million in a single year, which I also achieved several years later. So I'm speaking with authority and experience as I share these prosperity truths with you. And I tied my success into the greater good of the whole.

Here's the bottom line: Until you feel good about having money, and lots of it, you're unlikely to have it. The values and beliefs you have about money will determine how much of it you are eventually going to possess. Convince yourself of the importance of being successful. Don't allow yourself to entertain the thought of anything less.

Be inspired by those individuals who use money as a vehicle for social change, who make a difference.

Feel good about success, wealth and money. Let no one distort the value and importance of money with their negative views. Hold the vision clearly in your mind. To believe less is to handicap yourself and perhaps rob the world of whatever gifts you might have given to it but didn't because you held faulty, limiting beliefs. Desire to make a difference. One way of doing it is with your success.

Self-Talk

Something we were withholding made us
weak, until we found it was ourselves.

—ROBERT FROST

E ach of us has an inner voice that is talking to us all the time. And this inner voice isn't passive. It has very strong opinions on every aspect of our life. It's either encouraging us, or it's putting us down. It's either filling us with thoughts of confidence, hope and inspiration, or with thoughts of fear, worry and confusion. There doesn't seem to be a middle ground. So knowing what our inner voice is saying is important.

When you mentally repeat to yourself such phrases as, "I'll never do it," or "It'll be another disappointment for me," or "Things never go right," you are talking yourself into that exact situation. You begin to expect the worst and actually help it to occur. You are programming yourself to fail.

But the opposite kind of "self-talk" has an empowering effect. Phrases such as, "I can do it," or "I'm a champion," or "I always come through in the end," reinforce your belief in yourself. Positive self-talk gives you moral support. It's an inner cheering section that uplifts and encourages you.

PROGRAMMING YOURSELF FOR SUCCESS

I once spent a few days with an artist friend of mine. One morning, upon rising, he announced to me, "Today's the day one hundred things get done." He was behind on a number of his projects and had decided that this was to be an extremely productive day. So, throughout the day, he repeated to both himself and me that, "Today is the day one hundred things get done." I watched him condition his mind as he busily went from one assignment to another. Some took only a few moments, others a half-hour or more, but all the while he kept repeating his affirmation.

Now I don't know if he actually accomplished one hundred different chores, but by the end of the day, he had accomplished an unbelievable amount, and his self-talk had assisted him immeasurably.

You can use self-talk in any number of situations. Just find a statement that represents what you want to have happen to you in that situation and begin repeating it over and over to yourself, like a mantra. Do this while driving your car or waiting for an appointment or riding the elevator, and even while you're actually working.

A professional football player I know always says to himself whenever he gets the ball, "I'm unstoppable . . . I'm unstoppable," or "I'm a raging bull . . . I'm a raging bull." He repeats these phrases quickly, over and over to himself as he runs, and he claims it helps a lot. His statistics seem to verify that. Something's working for him, that's for sure.

Sam Butler, a salesman for a financial services firm who regularly finishes in the top 10 percent of his company, has the habit of saying to himself before he sees a client, "I'm going to make a great presentation." He takes two minutes to repeat this statement and makes a better presentation as a result.

Here's an incredible fact, and when you fully grasp the significance of it, it will change forever the way you talk to yourself: *You will come to believe whatever you repeat to yourself, providing you repeat it often enough.* Tell yourself enough times you're a loser and you'll believe it. Tell yourself over and over that you're destined for greatness and that's what you'll accept. And the most exciting part about all this is that you decide what you say. We can't stop the inner voice, but we can choose what it will say. We can make sure that it is a positive force in our life.

Scott Adams, creator of the hugely successful cartoon strip, *Dilbert*, is a great believer in affirmations. But rather than say them to himself he likes to write them out. When he was a struggling cartoonist he began to write out fifteen times every day, "I will be the most successful cartoonist in the world." No matter what happened or how disappointed he was, he made the time to follow through with this practice. It certainly worked. The struggling cartoonist is now indeed the most successful cartoonist in the world. As of 1998, he has an estimated 150 million readers in thirty-nine countries and the wildly popular *Dilbert* comic strip appears in more than 1,500 newspapers.

Whether your affirmations take the form of writing to yourself or speaking to yourself the principle is the same. You are choosing the thoughts that go through your mind.

Be selective with what you say to yourself and be vigilant. Negative self-talk almost always naturally follows a temporary failure or negative experience. Without our even realizing it, the inner voice begins saying, "It's hopeless," or "I'm a loser."

Knowing this, we can be on the lookout and catch ourselves quickly, as it happens.

Before my grandfather died I never missed a chance to get him talking about life. I loved his simple, honest, down-home philosophy and one conversation with him I remember particularly well. He was 103 at the time. "People respond so well to encouragement," he said to me, "yet most people continue to use criticism in trying to get people to change or do better. Why don't they use more encouragement?" How true, I thought, and let's remember this when we're dealing with ourselves as well. It's the same principle. We all need encouragement.

Don't be too hard on yourself. Be a good friend. If you want the best from yourself, feed yourself lots of encouragement. Ask yourself, "What can I say to myself today that is supportive and nurturing for me?"

"JUST MY LUCK"

How many times have you heard people use the expression, "It's just my luck" to explain away some misfortune? Have you ever heard someone use it positively? If not, then you've never been out sailing with Jim Burns. Jim is a jewelry wholesaler and a partner in my sailboat. We started using this expression half jokingly when sailing and, inevitably it seemed, we would encounter fine weather. "Just our luck," we would chime together, big grins on our faces as the wind propelled us along. Then I started using it in other areas of my life. Every time something good happened to me I found myself saying, "Just my luck!" It became a habit, a ritual. However, after a few months of doing this, something rather remarkable happened. I actually began thinking of myself as lucky, and as living a charmed life. Without even realizing what I was doing, I actually became what I was describing to myself—even though it was half in jest. And now, having imprinted this idea several thousand times, I really do think of myself as very lucky, and as a result of this belief wonderful, unexpected things continue to happen to me all the time.

Take this technique into your life and begin experimenting with its extraordinary power. Think of some empowering things you might say to yourself, and begin saying them. Be creative and have fun. Get your inner voice working for you.

A Success Vibration

Nothing succeeds like success.   —UNKNOWN

Success is not just an attitude; it is a vibration of energy and a very powerful vibration of energy. Those that possess it exude an aura of confidence that others are immediately aware of. A "success vibration" also naturally and effortlessly attracts more success to it. It has momentum and power that can be used again and again to great advantage. Those that understand this make it a habit to create and maintain a success vibration for themselves.

To create a success vibration, you simply start recognizing yourself as successful. You do this by regularly focusing on all the positive qualities you possess as well as your present and past achievements. Take time out right now to make a list of at least ten positive qualities about yourself. Don't just acknowledge the obvious, acknowledge everything. Include such things as, "I'm good at my job. I dress well. I'm a positive person. I'm creative." Don't feel silly or think it doesn't matter. Your positive qualities are just as real as the negative ones. Too often we put more emphasis on the negative part of us. Let's change this habit.

When you have your list, let your mind linger for several minutes on the success you already are. Go ahead and feel proud. Feel great. Feel successful. Do this for five minutes every day and you'll begin to build a success vibration.

Let every success you've ever achieved, both past and present, be a potential source of power for you. Often, when we accomplish something, we feel good about it for a few days, or if we're lucky, a few weeks. But then we move on to other matters. All too quickly we leave behind the feelings of accomplishment; we forget that we have even achieved them. We let go of and lose the success vibration that was created from our achievement. This is a complete waste of powerful "success energy." We can re-use success energies from past achievements again and again, with very positive results, but, unfortunately, we have never been taught how.

Focus regularly on all your achievements; even something that happened five or ten years ago can be used. But that's the past, you might say. True, it is the past, but the success energy produced by focusing on that achievement happens here in the present, and can assist you to further successes. So don't dismiss it.

Learn to pat yourself on the back often. Look for anything that makes you feel strong, victorious, successful, and good about yourself. Acknowledge anything and everything positive, and use it to create a vibration of success.

Sit down some time this week and take stock of your talents, your positive qualities, your market opportunities. Make a list of twelve reasons why you think you'll succeed at your goals. If you can think of a dozen reasons why you will succeed, and have them always in your mind, you'll never be intimidated by temporary setbacks, or when other people might try to discourage you. Refer to your list daily. Let this list empower you with confidence and energy. Keep adding to this list as new things come to you. Whenever you're feeling depressed or defeated, it will be like a safety net that catches you when you fall.

Success comes to those who become success-oriented. Failure comes to those who allow themselves to become failure conscious through neglect of positive reinforcement.

We all have successes and failures. We all have victories and defeats. Allow the failures and defeats to fade in memory, to go their way. Forget them. But your successes and victories should never be forgotten. They should be held onto and relived forever. Wear them within yourself like a victory banner, and let them empower you. They will always serve you well.

1) I'm capable with my hands.
2) I dress well when I want to
3) I succeed in my health in changing my diet
4) I'm kid like passioned about things and I thanfer them.
5) I made 300 K in making Bikes 15 years ago
6) I travelled a lot with confidence
7)

Don't Panic

*They say that time changes things, but actually
you have to change them yourself.*

—ANDY WARHOL

1	2	3	4	5	6
1	16	31	46	61	76
2	17	32	47	62	77
3	18	33	48	63	78
4	19	34	49	64	79
5	20	35	50	65	80
6	21	36	51	66	81
7	22	37	52	67	82
8	23	38	53	68	83
9	24	39	54	69	84
10	25	40	55	70	85
11	26	41	56	71	86
12	27	42	57	72	87
13	28	43	58	73	88
14	29	44	59	74	89
15	30	45	60	75	90

The preceding six columns each represent fifteen years in a ninety-year-old's life. Many people live to this age. My grandfather died when he was 107. He needed eight columns, not just six, to chart his life. So let's assume we're going to live a nice long, healthy life, and have a look at it.

Where are you on the chart? Halfway down the third column? End of the second? Beginning of the fourth? Circle your age and look at where you are on the chart. Get a feel for your whole life. Don't delude yourself into thinking your life is over when it's probably just beginning, or maybe halfway. I invented this chart many years ago to help me put my life in perspective during a very difficult period. It helped me immensely to take pressure off an arduous situation and realize how much time I still had available to me. I've shared it with many people since. It's good every now and then to put our life in perspective, rather than getting lost in the day-to-day details.

Just for fun, let's chart some of the people who have made fortunes in the marketplace. Steve Jobs, co-founder of Apple Computer, made his first million in the second column. So did Bill Gates of Microsoft. In fact, he made his first billion in the second column. However, most people who acquire fortunes reach their success in the third or fourth columns, or even later.

Eugene McDermott's little electronics store, which eventually became Texas Instruments, made him his first million in the third column. Edwin Land spent years painstakingly trying to develop a self-polarizing film, much to the ridicule and disbelief of people who knew it couldn't be done. But it could, and the Polaroid Corporation, which he founded, made him a huge fortune. This happened for him in the fourth column.

Mary Kay, a housewife with no business training who wanted to do something after her children had left home, founded Mary

Kay Cosmetics, which now has hundreds of millions of dollars a year in sales. Her success didn't begin until the fourth column as well.

Colonel Sanders of Kentucky Fried Chicken fame didn't reap financial rewards until the fifth column.

So don't panic and think life is passing you by. Relax and follow your game plan. There's lots of time yet to make your fortune.

Enthusiasm

A man can succeed at almost anything for
which he has unlimited enthusiasm.

—CHARLES SCHWAB

The word enthusiasm stems from the Greek word *enthous*, meaning "inspired," and that's exactly what happens when you are enthusiastic—you become inspired. Everything changes. Your whole being becomes charged in some inexplicable way, and you do things with the confidence of one who cannot fail. Your eyes sparkle, your words are powerful, minor day-to-day difficulties and annoyances are swept aside effortlessly. What's more, people who come in contact with you feel your enthusiasm. They are attracted and swayed by it. Enthusiasm is infectious and almost always magical in its ability to influence those around you.

This being the case, why don't more people avail themselves of this potent force? Maybe it's because most people wait to feel enthusiastic, rather than ever taking the steps to create enthusiasm. They are living the philosophy Woody Allen joked about when he wrote, "Life is 80 percent just showing up."

Enthusiasm is too important an asset to leave to chance. If you want it working for you, you should actively create it. When you're inspired by and excited about what you're doing, enthusiasm comes naturally. It becomes as if you're "on a mission" to accomplish your goal. So the more inspired and excited you can become about your goals, the more likely enthusiasm will surface. Enthusiasm is never forced; it comes from within. It comes from an inner conviction that what you are doing is good, valuable and important. The source of this enthusiasm comes from your thoughts and beliefs. Positive, inspiring thoughts about your life, your goals and your purpose will be fertile soil for enthusiasm. Anyone who consistently practices the activities set out in the following three lists will have enthusiasm working for them in whatever they do.

LIST 1: Ten reasons why it's good to be alive.

1. Having a wonderful companion
2. Having great friends
3. Enjoy the beauty of nature
4. Enjoy the beauty of Arts
5. Be free in this county to do anythings
6. Be excited about crafts
7. Be in good Health
8. Have a powerful mind that can do miracles
9. Enjoyed a quite time home
10. Enjoy good foods / physical pleasure

Too often we are overwhelmed with the day-to-day affairs of our lives. Stop for a few minutes every day and think about all the pleasures and joys that life affords you. Make a list and spend several minutes reminding yourself of the truth of what you've written. Acknowledge life's treasures. Friendship, nature, art, family, intellectual stimulation, passion, health, free will . . . On it goes. Take inventory, and each day remind yourself of these things until it becomes natural for you to remember and give thanks for them.

LIST 2: Ten reasons why it's advantageous for someone to have your product or service.

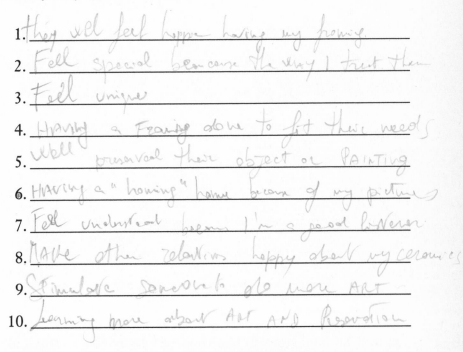

1. they will feel happier having my framing.
2. Feel special because the way I treat them
3. Feel unique
4. Having a Framing done to fit their needs
5. Well preserved their object or PAINTING
6. Having a "housing" home because of my pictures
7. Feel understood because I'm a good listener
8. Make other relations happy about my ceramics
9. Stimulate someone to do more ART
10. Learning more about ART AND Restoration

Become so excited about why people should have your product that you can't help but share it with them. Feel motivated by a mission to help people, to give them the opportunity to enjoy your product or service. It will become as if you are cheating them if you don't.

Then, when you're talking to others, the points you've written down will naturally and effortlessly flow into your conversation. People will become convinced because you are convinced. People will believe what you are saying because you sincerely believe it yourself.

LIST 3: Ten reasons why it's important that you are successful in life.

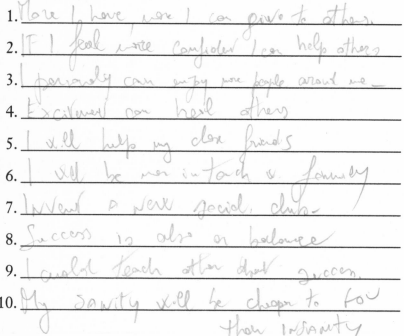

1. More I have more I can give to others
2. IF I feel more confident I can help others
3. I personally can enjoy more people around me
4. Excitement can heal others
5. I will help my close friends
6. I will be more in touch w family
7. Invent a new social club
8. Success is also a balance
9. I could teach other about success
10. My sanity will be cheaper to fou than insanity

Tie your success to a greater goal or mission. Be motivated to succeed. Remind yourself again and again why it's important to be successful. Remember, your success helps many people but your failure helps no one.

Study these lists every day until you have them memorized. Practice saying them aloud. Believe them absolutely. (If there are some points on your list that you still can't believe after a week of repeating them to yourself, take them off the list and replace them with something else.) The purpose of this process is to imprint these points into your consciousness.

Enthusiasm also opens the inner doors wide so that intuition freely flows to the conscious mind. While in this exalted state, you will find that you regularly receive new, inspiring ideas and brilliant hunches on how to achieve your goals. With enthusiasm you can accomplish almost anything. You can climb to heights you previously thought unattainable.

Opportunities Are Everywhere

Life is what happens to you while you're busy making other plans. —JOHN LENNON

Opportunities are everywhere; you just have to open your eyes to see them. But not your ordinary eyes. Your inner eyes, your intuition, sharpened and heightened by your conviction that opportunities are everywhere awaiting your discovery of them. Once you adopt this belief you will be amazed to find that opportunities do indeed exist in the most unusual places and in abundance.

A nine-year-old South African girl found one of the largest diamonds in the world. It was the size of a small fist and she found it beside a walkway that was passed by hundreds of people every day. There was something about that rock that made this little girl pick it up and take it to her father, who, having worked in the mines, suspected it might be more than just a "pretty rock." His suspicion was right, and after it was cut and polished, it was worth more than $2 million.

Chances are that you too wouldn't recognize a raw diamond if you saw one. A diamond in its natural state looks much different than when it's cut and polished and ready for mounting on a ring or pendant. So do raw opportunities. They seldom

look like the polished money-making ventures that savvy entrepreneurs turn them into.

Understand that opportunities are rarely announced by neon
signs that flash: "Opportunity. Opportunity. Here I am!" It
would be great if they did. But it's much more likely that they
are disguised as problems, difficulties, or seemingly inconsequential events. Opportunities exist in the most unusual places.
We don't see them because we haven't attuned ourselves to see
and expect them.

Let me share with you an incident that happened a number
of years ago on Easter morning. I hid some presents all around
my business manager's living room while she was still sleeping.
After she awoke I said I thought the Easter Bunny had arrived
and hidden some presents. She was thrilled and began looking
for them. After about fifteen minutes, she found three and
thanked me profusely. "There's more than that," I said, which
immediately had her searching again for more. She found a
couple more and we then sat down to breakfast. While we were
eating, I casually mentioned, "Too bad you didn't find the best
ones," with a mischievous look in my eye. "There's more?" she
asked incredulously. "There are ten." I announced. That was
all she needed to hear and, ignoring breakfast, she methodically
began going over the same area, but this time searching everywhere, looking into every nook and cranny. She looked in areas
she had previously searched, only this time she looked with eyes
that *knew* there were more presents out there. Nothing was
overlooked, and she eventually found all of them. It was lots of
fun, and we laughed about it for months. We still laugh about
it today when we think back on that incident, but there's an
important lesson to be learned here.

When I initially told her I had hidden some presents, she looked everywhere and finding three, stopped. When I informed her there were more she looked again and, finding two more, stopped again, although she had found only half the presents. It was only when I told her there were ten presents altogether that she methodically searched and searched until she found them all. Had I said nothing, she would have settled for the original three she'd found.

What are you settling for in your life? What are you being told? What do you believe? If you believe that there are no opportunities or very few opportunities left, chances are you won't find any. But if you believe that the times we live in are literally bursting with opportunities, you'll look till you find them.

At a charity fund-raising event, an associate of mine once had the good fortune of being seated at the same table as the oil billionaire John Paul Getty. A young man also at the table was lamenting the fact that all the good opportunities had been taken. There was no place for the big killing anymore. If only he'd been born thirty years earlier.

John Paul listened patiently and then felt the need to answer the young man. His words bear careful consideration. "Never have there been greater opportunities for success than there are today," spoke the great man. "The rapid growth of technology and the diversity of products and services now available will open up opportunities we can't even imagine today. There has never been a more exciting time to make money. Times of great change bring great opportunities, and these are times of great change." John Paul Getty died in 1978. If he thought things were changing rapidly in the late 1970s, imagine what he would say about today's rapidly changing business environment.

Fast-forward to 1998. Bill Gates, Microsoft's co-founder and the richest man in the world, echoes the same sentiments: "I think this is a wonderful time to be alive. There have never been so many opportunities to do things that were impossible before. It's the best time ever to start new companies and ventures."

All ages have had their share of people lamenting missed opportunities. There were those a hundred years ago who said all the good opportunities were gone. People said the same in the 1920s, the '30s, the '40s, the '50s. It's laughable of course, but each generation seems to feel that all the good opportunities have come and gone. What do you think they'll say about the late 1990s, and the early 2000s, twenty or thirty years from now? No opportunities? Who are you kidding? As of 1998 there are over 3 million millionaires in North America. How did they make their money? You'd be amazed. Here are three entrepreneurs who've made their millions by finding opportunities and following their instincts in places where others saw nothing.

Nipple rings, purple hair dye and black lipstick. You wouldn't think there was opportunity to make money here but there is—lots of it. Teenagers want it and Hot Topic's got it. "I dress this way to bother you," is the motto emblazoned across a T-shirt sold by Hot Topic, an upstart retail chain based in Pomona, California. The chain peddles nipple rings, tongue barbells, hair dye, T-shirts and hundreds of other items giving kids the means of expressing themselves. Morbid Metals, the company's line of body jewelry, is one of its more successful offerings.

Funky though the wares may be, there's nothing funky about the business's income. Hot Topic took in over $50 million last year. Orval Madden opened his first store in Los Angeles in 1989. Less than ten years later he has over 100 stores, and he expects to have 500 by the year 2007. The company went public in 1996 and the business was valued at close to $100 million, Orval's personal stake at a cool $10 million.

There's money to be made almost anywhere. How about making your fortune from bad breath—that's what Anthony Raissen did. His bad breath almost ruined his marriage. He experimented with mints, gums and candies, but they weren't strong enough. He tried parsley but couldn't bear the bitter aftertaste. During a trip to his native South Africa, Raissen met a group of chemists who had developed a formula of parsley seed and sunflower oil that worked like a charm. He bought the rights and returned to America to form Breath Asure Inc.

Raissen and his wife plotted a radical rollout: they launched Breath Asure at a garlic festival and were an immediate hit. Three years after its launch, Breath Asure is an $18 million company. Responding to the consumer, the company has just released another product, Pure Breath, a version of Breath Asure for dogs and cats. Don't laugh, they'll probably make a fortune with it as well. Opportunities are everywhere.

Former hedge-fund manager Jeff Bezos discovered opportunities are everywhere when he left his successful, high-paying job to create one of the great World Wide Web success stories. He founded Amazon.com, a virtual bookstore with over 2 million titles. Innovative marketing and such features as chats with authors and readers' reviews proved highly successful. A blend of selection and "community" helped his privately held Amazon.com pull in estimated sales of close to $20 million in 1996. The next year he went public and became a millionaire many times over.

These are just three examples of the millions of people who have turned new and unusual ideas into fortunes. Why not you?

One final word about opportunities before I leave the subject (and I hope this will put to rest the myth of no opportunities out there once and for all). Every time you find yourself thinking there are no opportunities around, remind yourself of this indisputable fact: There are people who haven't been born yet who will one day make great fortunes, in the stock market, in real estate, who will climb to the top of the very industry where you now find yourself employed. These intrepid individuals will start new businesses that no one has ever thought of before. This will in turn pioneer still new industries that will create even more opportunities. It never stops.

There will be men and women who will rise to be the leaders and champions in business, sports and the arts. There will be social activists who will make breakthroughs in crime, poverty, the environment. So, if they can do it, and they aren't even born yet, what about you? What's your excuse? Don't you, in fact, have a head start on them? Think about it. They aren't even born yet!

Program your mind to believe that opportunities are everywhere in abundance. Develop the eyes and instincts to recognize these opportunities when they appear. Do this and you'll be amazed at what you'll find.

Find Your Passion

This above all,—to thine own self be true ...
—SHAKESPEARE

A recent national poll revealed that more than 80 percent of North America's working population do not enjoy the work they do. This is a profoundly tragic statistic, considering that work consumes so much of our lives. Nor is it a good formula for success, because when you study closely people who are successful it becomes abundantly clear that their achievements are directly related to the enjoyment they derive from their work.

This really struck home for me while I was writing this book. Since this is a book about money and success, I decided to send each of my financially successful friends (those with assets over $1 million) a copy of the manuscript so that I could get their feedback. As I finished my list and was reading over the names, I suddenly realized that every single one of them had achieved their success in areas they enjoyed working in—one was in publishing, another was a jewelry wholesaler, one in law, still another in home renovating—and so it went. They had found their passion, devoted themselves to it and had prospered. Every single one of them was doing what they loved doing.

It got me thinking: Has anybody ever made a fortune doing what he or she dislikes? I thought about it for a while and you know what? I couldn't think of anyone. Not one. This is something to seriously ponder if you presently find yourself trying to get ahead working at an occupation you dislike.

DO WHAT YOU LOVE; THE MONEY WILL FOLLOW

Lars-Eric Lindblad loves traveling. As he backpacked his way to some of the more exotic locations around the world, he thought of what he would do when he eventually returned home. Nothing seemed appealing; and then he suddenly had an idea. "There are probably others like myself," he thought, "who want to experience a more adventurous type of travel. Why not start a business to cater to their specific needs?" So that's what he did. He started his own travel agency, Lindblad Travel, offering adventurous trips to offbeat locations—the Gobi Desert, Antarctica, the Galapagos Islands. People in the travel industry told him he was sure to fail. "You can't make money offering just adventure packages," they said, almost unanimously. This was before exotic travel became fashionable. Lars was one of the first to venture into this field and succeed he did, in a very big way. And 500,000 customers later, his travel business is still booming. Here's the lesson for those of you who wish to follow your dream: the real key to Lindblad's success is that he chose something that he was excited about, something he believed in.

Peter Moore hated his job as a bank manager. Although he liked dealing with people, he felt stuck in his choice of occupations and felt he wasn't using his talents to the maximum. He wanted more. Realizing that his people skills would be well suited to sales, he began thinking of a career in selling. But selling what? Then one day, as he was handling the affairs of a woman whose husband had recently died, it hit him. Why not sell life insurance?

Peter's experience as a bank manager had given him experience in dealing with families who are left without proper financial support. He believed absolutely in the service and excitedly began researching all the available companies to see which ones had the best policies. When he had made his decision, he approached the sales manager and told him what he'd done and why he wanted to sell life insurance for them. He was given a job on the spot.

Within one year he became one of their top salesmen, and eventually he became their district sales manager for the entire West Coast. He succeeded because he found something he could do with conviction. Something that felt right. He found his passion.

Stephen Sandler thought his grandmother's mustard was the best in the world. Nothing else he had ever tasted even came close. Everyone else who tasted it at his house said the same. Then, one day, he had a wild idea. "Why not bottle it and sell it?" But then came the doubts. "There are already lots of brands of mustard available. I have no real business experience. There's stiff competition for shelf space. Why would they give an unknown a chance?" And there were hundreds of other reasons why not to do it. But Stephen genuinely believed his grandmother's mustard was better than anything else available, and this thought kept nagging at him. So he decided to give it a try.

He made twelve jars, had some labels printed, and went to visit several local delicatessens. He told them he already had a company that produced the mustard and offered them a free jar as a sample. Much to his surprise, Stephen received an order for 120 jars from one of them.

"At six jars an hour," he laughed, "I didn't think I'd ever get through that first order." He started by making it in his own kitchen and eventually the operation took over the house. Then he had to move to larger premises. Sandler Mustard is now sold in delicatessens all across the country and his small company, just barely out of its infancy, is now worth over $2 million. Stephen Sandler found his passion—mustard—and he made it his livelihood.

"People whose whole objective is making money, usually don't," says Jerry White, professor of entrepreneurial studies at the University of Toronto, Canada. He should know. He's made it his business to study successful entrepreneurs and to teach others their winning ways, and the one message that came through loud and clear in his research was: Find a product or service you can believe in passionately, because without this you will not succeed.

What is your calling? To what areas are you best suited? How can you find a livelihood that will nourish and fulfill you?

You start by simply believing in yourself. Take stock of your assets, your strong points, and then see how you can best use them. Very often it's a lack of self-confidence that keeps us in positions we don't like. If this is the case then embark upon a daily program designed to build self-confidence. Make this your first priority, and once this is achieved, your perspectives too will change.

WHO AM I? WHAT ARE MY POSSIBILITIES?

You may think of yourself as a parent or spouse or in terms of your present job or profession, but that is only a part of who you are. Beyond this what are your possibilities? You have talents and strengths. You have natural inclinations towards certain subjects, while others have no interest to you. You have activities that bring you pleasure and others that you disdain. In fact you are quite unique, and this uniqueness can be your compass. Trust it and let it lead you.

Remind yourself that you possess a powerful subconscious mind that will guide you. Go to it daily, instructing it to bring you the answers you are looking for.

Make Lists:

♦ Write down all the activities that give you pleasure.

♦ Write down your mental assets and strengths, your past and present accomplishments.

♦ Write down choices that you would make for yourself if money were not an issue and careers that sound interesting regardless of whether you think you have the talent or opportunity to pursue them.

Open up your mind to options and possibilities. Dare to dream. There are no boundaries except those that exist in your mind. As media tycoon Rupert Murdoch said, "Fortune favors the bold."

The choice of how to make a living is perhaps the single most important of all our decisions, yet it's often the one most neglected. Sometimes we feel we have to take a job because of financial needs, or we are steered into a career because it has "excellent prospects," when really our heart isn't in it. This is unfortunate and totally unnecessary when you realize how many options are available to you. Certainly in any given period of several months or even several years you might have to work at something you don't enjoy to make ends meet, to pay off debts or just to get started, but new opportunities will always present themselves to you if you are open and receptive to them. Don't ever sell yourself short. You deserve more than just a job.

No amount of money, no matter how much it is, will ever compensate you sufficiently for remaining in a job that is drudgery and robs you of your spirit, or one that prevents you from fulfilling a dream. As the old saying goes, "In your haste to make a living don't forget to make a life." Be bold; forge off in a direction that you have a passion for.

That's exactly what Dominic Chang did. An avid golfer, he often felt guilty about putting golf ahead of his family, and he suspected millions of other golfers felt the same way. So in 1992 he quit his job at the Bank of New York, where he was a senior vice-president, to follow his instinct and passion. He raised the money to open Family Golf Centers Inc. The basic tenet of his business plan: Encourage golfers to bring their spouses and children along with them to the centers. Have party rooms, snack bars, restaurants, miniature golf, so that it is exciting for everyone to come, male, female, young and old. His first center was a big hit and was soon followed by others. Now his company has gone public and Dominic's three million shares are worth close to $100 million. Not bad for six years worth of work, or should I say six years of passion.

Everyone has his or her own specific vocation or mission in life. It cannot be replaced by something else, nor can someone else do it for you. Everyone's task is to discover his or her uniqueness and find an opportunity to implement it.

Life is filled with choices and opportunities, so follow your heart, your instinct. Find something you can be passionate about and devote yourself to it. This is where your personal fulfillment as well as your contribution to the world lies.

Joseph Campbell says it well: "Your whole physical being

knows that this [following your passion] is the way to be alive in this world and the way to give to the world the very best that you have to offer. There is a track just waiting there for each of us, and once on it, doors will open that were not open before and would not open for anyone else."

"Every calling is great when greatly pursued," said Oliver Wendell Holmes. Whether you're selling life insurance, designing buildings, managing a company, writing a book, marketing new products or cutting hair, find the passion and excitement in it. If you can, you will succeed like you never have before. Follow your dream. Trust your instincts. Find that something you can believe in passionately and give it your all. Do what you love; the money will follow.

PART II
◆ ◆ ◆
ACTION

Waking Up in the Age of Information

Toto, I have a feeling we're not in Kansas anymore. —DOROTHY (FROM THE WIZARD OF OZ)

We are living in one of the most exciting periods civilization has ever known. As futurist Laurence Frank states, "We are living the events which for centuries to come will be minutely studied by scholars who will undoubtedly describe these days as probably the most exciting and creative in the history of mankind." We have given it a name, this astounding time; we call it the information age, and it's more than just a catch phrase. It consists of millions of events happening simultaneously which, in the process, are redefining and shaping the way we work and live. It is a period of stupendous and radical change.

It's staggering how quickly it's all happening. You can now fly from New York to London on the Concord, crossing the Atlantic in barely three hours while e-mailing your office with instructions, and communicating with your wife via the cell phone. Meanwhile you're traveling faster than the speed of sound. And what's incredible is that we take it all for granted.

Technology is redefining our lives, and it's happening at warp speed. This unprecedented upsurge of information and knowledge-based technology is expanding exponentially.

Change now takes place in nanoseconds, and this change is happening everywhere.

AT&T handles approximately 3 billion transactions an hour. There are over 100 million trades completed each day on the world's stock markets via the Internet. The 250-channel TV is here.

Microprocessors run at a billion cycles a second. A microchip the size of your thumbnail can hold as much information as a library. Forget typing, computers are now voice-activated, following your verbal instructions, even going so far as to recognize your voice and refusing to work for those voices it isn't familiar with.

Global Positioning Systems (GPS) that use satellite receivers to calculate locations, originally used only by the U.S. Defense Department to plot troop movements, are now found in sailboats. Electronic maps are scheduled to be standard equipment in automobiles. Soon after they could well be as small and common as wristwatches.

Biologists have cracked the genetic code and now understand the language of genes. With this new technology and knowledge they can splice genes, clone species, create new antibodies and mutations, and that's just the beginning. Tailored viruses, cellular grafting, artificial glands and organs are all on their way.

Somewhere during this decade we found ourselves living in the future. Its arrival is both thrilling and overwhelming. Thrilling because of the tremendous opportunities it presents us, and overwhelming because it necessitates that we redefine who we are and where we're going. The old rules don't apply anymore.

For example, the idea of one career in a lifetime is as outdated as the dial phone (remember them?). Anyone who wants to keep pace with these changes and take advantage of the new opportunities they present needs to readdress the whole notion of work. To survive and prosper in the new millenium means to change, learn and constantly re-invent yourself. Author Alvin Toffler puts it more bluntly: "The illiterate of the 21st century will not be those who cannot read and write but those who cannot learn, unlearn and relearn."

Charles Darwin's "survival of the fittest" is as appropriate today as it has always been. However, let me first clear up a common misunderstanding of what he meant by "survival of the fittest." Darwin did not mean "fittest" in the sense of the strongest or most domineering, as is commonly thought. He meant that the best possible fit between organism and environment is the one that survives and succeeds. And the organism that fits best is the one that is most capable of adapting and using its strengths to meet the challenges presented to it.

If we are then to be the fittest in today's rapidly changing marketplace, we need to rethink our present situation carefully and begin equipping ourselves with new talents and skills. In the 21st century, the fittest will be those who can adapt and change, those who can obtain the information they need and learn skills quickly, as required.

Knowledge is indeed power and, in these times, even more so. Thomas Spencer, a behavioral psychologist, has said, "The average worker of today will probably have to relearn his job five different times in his career." And he could be underestimating it significantly. Marshall McLuhan put it another way: "The future of work now consists of learning a living rather than earning a living."

You hear it again and again in every industry; the message is loud and clear: "Learning new skills is the key that will unlock the door to the opportunities of the future."

If indeed this is the case, and all the indicators point in this direction, then the most important question you can ever ask yourself, and you should ask it of yourself today, is, "What do I need to learn?" If you do, and you act intelligently, you will be well positioned for the enormous array of opportunities that change is bringing. Not only will you survive; you will enjoy tremendous success.

Choices

Choice, not chance, determines destiny.

—UNKNOWN

Are you fully aware of the countless choices that you make each and every day? Probably not. Few of us ever stop to consider the multitude of options available to us. Too often we fall into routines where we feel restricted and confined by our present circumstances. This is unfortunate because the problem lies not with your life situation, but with your perception of it. I can assure you, without even knowing who you are, that there are numerous choices you could make that would radically change the direction of your life. I know this because every life contains a myriad of choices and options at every single junction of time. Right this very moment you have choices that if pursued would lead you on the path to success and happiness. Increase your awareness of your choices and you will automatically enjoy a new sense of freedom in your life. You can start by becoming aware that choice itself is one of the basic foundations of your life.

Stop for a moment and think of some of the choices you have already made. You have chosen where you live. You have chosen your present occupation. You have chosen the friends you associate with. You have chosen the clothes you wear and you have chosen the particular outfit you have on today. You have chosen to read this particular book and you have chosen to read it now. There are more choices in your life than you are aware of. In fact your life is filled with choices. Some of them are made with great deliberation; most are made unconsciously, without our realizing we're making them. The trick is to become conscious of our choices. The ability to choose and direct our life is not to be taken for granted, or overlooked. Yet listen to the way people normally talk. It's as if they have no freedom or choice at all:

"I have to go to a meeting this weekend."

"I have to stay home and look after the kids."

"I have to work at a job I don't like."

"I have to go to the store and buy some bread."

"I have to pay the mortgage each month."

"I have to . . . I have to . . . I have to . . . ."

How many times do you hear it said? How many times in a day do you say it yourself? Mostly it's unconscious, yet it has its effect. You're programming your mind to believe that you have no choices, that you're forced into doing something that you don't want to do. That's a very dangerous imprint, especially since it's not true. Everything you do is because of choice.

I have to go to a meeting this weekend really means you choose to go to the weekend meeting. "No," you might reply, "that's the last thing I want to do but it's mandatory for everyone. I have to go."

No—you choose to go. You could choose not to go. Perhaps that would mean phoning your boss and explaining why you won't be there, coming up with a really creative reason. Maybe you phone in sick. You could quit your job. There are always choices.

Really, what you should be saying is, "I choose to go to the meeting rather than explain why I didn't show," or "I choose to go to the meeting rather than risk the ramifications of not going." But you have in fact chosen to go regardless of why you have chosen to do so—it was a choice and you made it.

Let me share with you a conversation I had recently with a student at one of my seminars.

"I have to stay home and look after the kids," she said.

"You have to?"

"Yes, they are both preschoolers. One is four, the other two. I have to stay home with them."

"Don't you have the choice of daycare?"

"My husband and I both believe the children need a parent full time in these early years, so I have to stay home."

"I respect your decision, but really it's a choice. You've chosen to stay home with them."

"Yes, that's what I said."

That's not what she said, and that's not what her subconscious mind was picking up from her.

How you perceive your situation, how you frame it in your mind is important. It's not simply a matter of semantics; it's a matter of what you're imprinting into your subconscious. To be conscious of your choices and to choose with awareness is far different from plodding ahead unconsciously thinking you have no options in life. One is exhilarating and empowering. The other is restrictive and causes you to feel helpless and stuck. Unfortunately most of us have fallen into the habit of the latter. But we can choose to change this habit. We don't *have to* remain stuck. We can choose new habits of perception.

Every time you find yourself thinking or saying, "I have to . . .", catch yourself saying it, and then stop for a moment and consciously do a little one-minute exercise. Examine your options. How many exist? Use your imagination. Come up with as many options as you possibly can in one minute. Be creative. Have fun with it. Watch how it empowers you and gives you energy literally within seconds of those other options appearing. Suddenly you don't have to . . . you choose to.

For example you catch yourself saying, "I have to go to the store and buy a loaf of bread." Now examine your options. You could go back to the fridge, check what's there and decide to make something besides sandwiches. You could announce to the family that everyone is fasting tonight. You could order in some food. You could go out to a restaurant. You could phone a friend, invite her over and ask her to do you a favor and pick up some bread on her way. There are lots of choices. Then, after weighing all these choices, if you still want to go to the store and buy bread, rephrase your statement. "I choose to go to the store to buy some bread." What a difference this practice will make to your life. Firstly, to preface each action with "I choose to . . . ." makes you feel that your life is filled with choices, which in fact it is. Secondly, it will open your eyes to see many other options and choices you had previously been blind to. You will find yourself being more creative, bold and adventurous. Do this exercise every day and it will literally transform your life.

Goals

Life is either a daring adventure, or it is
nothing. —HELEN KELLER

I love sailing. I have a beautiful 32-foot wooden schooner that was hand-built by a friend of mine who is a master West Coast craftsman. I go out in it as often as possible. Sometimes I'll take the boat out in the afternoon and just sail around the harbor, back and forth, enjoying the sun and wind in my face. I don't end up going anywhere, but that's because I'm sailing just for the sake of sailing.

Other times I'll take off for a week or more. Occasionally, even for a month or two. At these times I have a clearly defined destination. Each day I study the charts carefully before I begin and set myself a course for the day. I navigate. I choose and trim the sails according to wind conditions, correct my bearing and make changes as necessary. I watch for and recognize signs along the way, a reef here, an island there; at each point of the journey I try to establish both where I am and where I'm going. I can't imagine doing it any other way. It can't be done any other way. Imagine sailing off with no charts or no course, just with hope and determination that you will arrive. How ridiculous, and yet that's what we do when we head off in life, hoping and wanting the best but setting no goals as to how to achieve it. Is it any wonder we don't arrive?

"The reason most people don't achieve their goals in life," remarked author and lecturer Dennis Waitley, rather dryly, "is because they didn't have any in the first place." Everyone wants to be healthy, happy, successful and hundreds of other things, but not everyone has goals that map out how they will achieve these objectives.

ARE YOU LIKE ALICE IN WONDERLAND?

In Lewis Carrol's classic *Through the Looking Glass*, one scene has Alice completely lost, not knowing which way to turn, so she asks the Cheshire cat, perched comfortably on a tree limb, for some help.

"Would you tell me, please, which way I ought to go from here?" asks Alice.

"That depends a good deal on where you want to get to," replies the cat.

"I don't much care where," says Alice.

Then it doesn't much matter which way you go," comes the reply.

"So long as I get somewhere," Alice adds in explanation.

"Oh, you're sure to do that," grins the cat.

I love that. It's so absurd and yet all too similar to the way we often live our lives. We make a tragic error when we mistake working hard and being busy with achieving goals. We assume that if we're working hard we must be getting ahead. But working hard and trying to get ahead without specific, clearly defined goals on how to get there is living in a fool's paradise. And the sooner we recognize this, the better.

WHAT DO YOU WANT OUT OF LIFE?

What do you want out of life? Do you know? If you're not sure it's probably time for some serious self-reflection. Each of us at certain times in our life need to stop and take stock of where we are and where we are going, to make certain that the direction our life is moving in is the direction we want.

The goals you set for yourself will determine the circumstances and situations you will meet in life. This being so, choose wisely and pursue those things that are closest to your heart. I'm reminded of the saying, "A man climbed the ladder of success only to discover it was against the wrong wall." Don't make wrong choices in your life. Your goals should reflect your passions, your instincts, your vision.

A poet once wrote:

One ship drives east, another west
By the selfsame winds that blow.
'Tis the set of the sails and not the gales,
That tell us the way to go.

Your goals, when pursued, set your sails and determine the direction you will go.

If you find yourself unclear on your own goals, set aside half an hour a day for at least a month. Give yourself this time. Don't rush it. Each day, make a list of the five most important things you want to achieve in your life. Do this every day. The reason I say every day is that your list will change from day to day. Some items will seem important one day and not so important the next. Others will be repeated over and over. Doing this over a one-month period will make it possible for you to separate temporary desires from those that are truly important to you.

Here's another method that will help you. Imagine you're

ninety years old, looking back at your life. What would you like
to have seen happen? What would you regret most not doing?
This exercise can help you get a clear picture of what you really
want to do.

HAVE LARGE GOALS

I discovered the power of large goals first-hand as I was about
to embark on my first lecture tour of Australia many years ago.
I was in Thailand when I phoned the Australian promoter who
was organizing the tour. We had made an arrangement that she
was to receive 20 percent of the profits for her work. I casually
mentioned that I thought she would be making about $10,000
a month plus expenses. I thought she'd be very pleased. You can
imagine my surprise when she said that wasn't enough; what
she needed to make was $20,000 a month, and that's what she
was counting on.

I didn't know what to say. I knew the reality of the situation
and what we'd probably be earning. I'd been in the business for
many years and for her to earn $20,000 a month, I would have
to make more than double what I'd ever made previously. I knew
that was impossible.

I wrestled with this for several days. What were my options?
I could pay her more and take a smaller percentage myself, or
she could settle for $10,000. After all, it was a considerable
wage. Nothing felt right until I realized that maybe, just maybe,
it was indeed possible to make more money in Australia than I
had anticipated.

I will forever remember the exact moment that this thought
came into my mind, because it marks a turning point in my life.
I was walking along the beach, while the sun was setting, when
I suddenly thought, why not make twice as much money? It

would solve the problem perfectly. I had until this point thought it was impossible, but something within me now said it was possible. And as the thought of earning twice as much money became a possibility in my mind, I became charged in a way I'd never experienced before. I felt more powerful than the setting sun. I was unexpectedly alive in a whole new way.

Over the next two weeks, as I walked the beaches, new ideas, new ways of marketing myself, new plans kept flooding into my mind. What had been totally impossible two weeks earlier was now not only possible, but even probable—if I followed my plan. I couldn't believe the change.

We arrived in Australia and I had the most successful lecture tour of my career. The promoter got her $20,000 a month for the duration of the tour, and I earned more money than I'd ever made in my life.

However, I received something more valuable than the money. I learned that opportunities open up when you open up your thoughts. I knew this not as a concept, but as a reality. I had just watched it work for me in the most incredible way. Large goals have a momentum and power that give you the means to achieve them. Don't waste your time asking yourself, "How am I going to do it? How will it happen?" Just make the decision to do it and then watch the ideas and plans follow.

Patanjali, author of *The Yoga Sutras*, and one of the founders of yoga in ancient India, put it this way: "When you are inspired by some great purpose, some extraordinary project, all your thoughts break their bonds. Your mind transcends limitations; your consciousness expands in every direction in a new, great and wonderful world. Dormant forces, faculties and talents become alive, and you discover yourself to be a greater person by far than you ever dreamed yourself to be."

Work Smart Not Hard

*If we did all the things we are capable of
doing, we would literally astonish ourselves.*

—THOMAS EDISON

There is a common fallacy about work that is the cause of much confusion and undue hardship, namely: The harder you work, the more successful you will be.

If you believe this, then in order to be more successful you will need to work harder. This is what most people are now doing in their lives. They are taking on more projects, working longer hours, neglecting their families and health and getting stressed about it in the process. They are in fact working so hard that they don't have a chance to be successful. How could they be? The premise is all wrong.

Stop for a minute and think about it. If it's true that the harder you work the more successful you are, then that should mean the hardest working people are the most successful. Look around you—often the hardest working people in our society are the poorest paid. How can this be?

Does the writer who writes twenty books necessarily make more money than the one who writes two? What if none of the twenty get published? What if both books by the writer who writes two become bestsellers? Does the publisher, reader or reviewer care how hard the writer works? Is it a factor? Is a book that takes ten years to write always better than one that is written effortlessly in three months with a flash of inspiration? If I work harder than Bill Gates will I be more successful than Bill Gates? If you work harder and longer than me will you be more successful than me? Is hard work really the magic formula to success?

It's time to wake up and shake off the shackles of this incredibly harmful belief. It's time to realize it's not how hard you work but how smart you work!

Never measure how hard you're working. This dimension is meaningless. If you're working hard it can lull you into believing you're being effective. Measure how smart you're working. Ask yourself, "Am I using my time and resources to the best of my ability?" "Am I working smart or am I just plain working hard?" And know how to tell the difference between the two. Never confuse them.

There is a Zen story about a student who came to the Zen master and asked, "What is Zen?" The master answered, "When we work, we work. When we eat, we eat. When we sit, we sit. When we sleep, we sleep. That's Zen."

"But doesn't everybody do that?" asked the student?

"No," replied the master. "It takes practice to do it."

Working smart takes practice too. Never confuse putting in time with effective work. If we spend twelve hours at the office we think we worked twelve hours. We feel either satisfied or drained, depending on our perspective, but did we work smart? Perhaps if we were organized, relaxed and in the flow, we could have done the same work in six hours. It's entirely possible.

Is the salesman who makes the most sales calls the one who does best? Is it the number of calls you make that makes the difference? Is making twenty sales calls always more effective than making fifteen? What about the quality of the lead? How much time did you spend with the customer listening to her concerns and explaining the benefits of your product or service? Were you relaxed, confident, in the flow, or just going through the motions? How well did you research and prepare? Maybe you were pre-occupied with a personal matter and couldn't really get into your work. Maybe you were just working hard and not smart.

When you finish your workweek, never ask yourself how hard you worked. That's irrelevant. Ask yourself how smart you worked. Did I use my time in the best possible way? Was I creative? Productive? These are the questions you want answered.

A TASK WILL ALWAYS EXPAND TO FILL THE AMOUNT OF HOURS YOU DEVOTE TO IT

Arthur C. Clarke, a prolific author best known for his book *2001: A Space Odyssey*, which was made into a hugely successful motion picture, learned this first-hand when he was told by his physician he had less than a year to live. Walking out of the doctor's office into the busy streets of London, he had several serious matters to consider. It was not so much his life he was concerned about, but that of his wife and young children. How would they make out financially when he was gone? What was he leaving them? The money he made as an author was always sufficient providing he kept writing, but with less than a year he didn't have much time.

Normally he took approximately a year and a half to write a book. But even that much was impossible now with these new time restraints that life had cruelly placed upon him. So he made a decision. He would write six books within the next year. Two months for each book, and from the royalties of these books his family would at least have a financial cushion to fall back on. How he would write a book in two months when it normally took him eighteen he didn't know, but somehow he would do it. He would do it because he had to. It was a decision that would change his life.

Here the story takes a strange twist, much the same as in his own novels. As the adage says, truth is often stranger than fiction. Clarke indeed wrote six new novels, and in the process of this accomplishment something remarkable happened. He somehow managed to completely cure himself of his illness. A year later there was no sign of it, but in the meantime he had formed the habit of writing a book in two months. Did he go back to spending eighteen months on a book now that he had the time? Would you? "I liked my new productivity," he said. "And you know what? I think I write better this way."

I have noticed that successful men and women have the uncanny knack of getting things done quickly and effectively. Not once in a while or when a deadline is looming, but consistently and regularly. They know how to work smart. It's one of the reasons they are so successful.

There's another old saying: "If you want something done give it to a busy person," and it's true. A busy person is in the flow of getting things done, lots of things. He or she knows how to prioritize. How to work effectively. How to surmount obstacles and not get distracted. They work smart. Not only that but they usually get things done in half or a quarter of the time it takes others. You too can find this rhythm and make it work for you. So if you have a hundred tasks in front of you, don't despair. Prioritize. Give yourself a time limit and find the flow and rhythm to accomplish them all. You'll be more effective and you'll be more relaxed doing it. Don't think "work hard," think "work smart." One approach brings you success; the other simply makes you tired.

Three Winning Strategies

Management is doing things right; leadership is doing the right things. —PETER DRUCKER

STRATEGY 1
Start with the End in Mind

Each day of your life should contribute in a meaningful way to the vision you have of your life as a whole. To begin with the end in mind means always having a clear picture of your ultimate destination. What do you want to see happening in your life ten years from now? Twenty-five years from now? Be very clear and aware of what your financial, spiritual, business and health goals are. You need to be very clear about your ultimate objectives in order to design a strategy to take you there.

Starting with the end in mind means using your imagination to work backwards, seeing all the steps needed to take you to your goal. When you know where you're going, there are very clear signposts at every stage of your journey to success. Know what your signposts are so you can accurately assess where you are and how you are doing. This is where your imagination can help you. Working backwards from where you want to be, and seeing the steps that take you there gives you a blueprint to follow. What needs to be done then becomes less of a mystery.

99

Keep this overall image in your mind. It will both inspire and remind you why you're doing specific tasks. It will keep you on track.

STRATEGY 2
Organize and Execute Around Priorities

How can I be most effective with the time I have available to me? This is the question each of us must address each day. Your time and energy are limited. You cannot do a thousand things in a day, although there are probably a thousand things that could be done that would be helpful to you. You need to make decisions on what actions are more important than others, and in what order you will do them.

This involves managing yourself and using your time wisely. Time Management is a misnomer. You don't manage time. Time is a constant; you manage and organize yourself, and in doing so you initiate actions which produce results. Business is a matter of "getting things done." Organize and execute around priorities. Have a hierarchy of what needs to be done. Break it down into smaller parts. See clearly the whole picture. The macro- and micro-view. The overview and the details. Don't let the details take over. Taking a week or two to design a brochure when you allotted only a couple of days might produce a great brochure, but from a macro view was it the best use of your time? Another way of looking at this is to ask yourself what didn't get done, what was ignored because I spent this time on the brochure? Make sure you like the answers you're getting.

Don't be pennywise and pound-foolish. This old English proverb is wise council. You spend three afternoons shopping around to find the cheapest color photocopier and you save $200. Which is great, but unless your time is worth less than

$15 an hour might you not have spent your time better? Use your time where it will produce the best results for you. And the decision as to where you will spend your time is not made by asking yourself what do I enjoy doing most, but rather what will be the most effective use of my time. How can I be most productive today? This week? This month? Ask yourself these questions and follow through with the actions that are appropriate.

STRATEGY 3
Plan Your Work, Work Your Plan

How many times have you heard a coach of a professional sports team explain a loss to the media in this way: "We didn't follow our game plan."?

Well why on earth would they not follow their game plan if that's what they intended to do? Because it's easy to stray off course. In the excitement and pressure of each play unfolding, you make decisions on the spur of the moment, sometimes in a split second. You get so caught up in the action that's happening right in front of you, you forget the original game plan and simply react.

So too in business. Often it becomes a "fix what's in front of me right now" affair. Phone calls, deadlines, changing priorities, unforeseen developments, emergencies, new opportunities, all have a way of sidetracking you from your original plan.

Knowing this, it's important that you always have an overview of what you want to accomplish each week, each month, each year, and that you plan your work and work your plan to achieve it.

Sure, you'll still have the phone calls, deadlines and new developments clamoring for your attention but, if you follow this simple four-step plan, you'll find you can easily correct your course when you get sidetracked, and move quickly and effectively towards your goals.

STEP 1
Make a List

Write down what needs to be accomplished this week, what phone calls, letters, actions will move you forward in your goals. Who do you need to see? What do you need to do? What new information could you obtain that would help you? What can you do to create more opportunities? What would make this a productive, successful workweek? Design a weekly list that moves you aggressively towards your goals.

STEP 2
Do It

Whatever can be done immediately—do it! What else can be done today? Do it! And, one by one, you begin accomplishing what's on your list. As the Russian mystic Gurdjieff so wisely advised: "Don't think of results, just do." Let action be your vehicle to success. Accomplish everything you put on your list. Let this be your top priority.

Now, you might find that new developments will happen during your week and you want to add tasks to your list. That's fine, add them, but never—and I repeat—never, under any circumstances, delete items from your list (unless they have been accomplished). The only time for deletion of an unfinished task is at the end of the week, during your review time. This is an important rule to follow, as it gets you into the habit of following through with your plan.

STEP 3
Review Your Actions

This is a step that most people omit in their work plans, and that's a critical error. Reviewing your week is just as important as planning your week. In fact you should spend twice as much time reviewing your week as you do planning it, because this is how you find out what's really happening with your work. Plans and good intentions are useless unless they are followed up by effective action. Reviewing will reveal much to you.

In reviewing you need to ask yourself lots of questions:
- What was accomplished?
- What wasn't? Why?
- What new developments occurred?
- What did I learn?
- What needs to be done next?
- What am I not doing enough of? Why?
- How can I be more effective?

Analyze and review last week's actions thoroughly before you plan your next week's activity. Remember, reviewing in many ways is even more important than planning. Take your time and find out what happened, what didn't and why, before you move ahead.

STEP 4
Make Another List

From the analysis and insights you obtained during Step 3, put together a new list for the upcoming week.

When these four steps are followed regularly, two important things happen. First, lots of work gets accomplished, and this is important. Second, and this is equally important, you'll uncover patterns of behavior in yourself that you never knew existed. In reviewing your list week after week, you'll discover how you consistently avoid certain types of tasks. This is a revealing and sobering realization. However, knowing this will assist you greatly in making the internal changes necessary to your becoming more effective.

Remember, knowing what to do and actually doing it are two totally different steps. There's nothing radically new in what I've proposed here; you probably know much of this system already. But that's just the first step. The second, more important step, is that of actually doing it. Action, rather than words, is what will make a difference. If you can enact these strategies, week after week, month after month, you'll be well on your way to far greater success in your life.

Learn to Love
the Word "No"

After the final no, there comes a yes.

—WALLACE STEVENS

There is a famous line in Francis Ford Coppola's *Apocalypse Now*, the classic film that is a brilliant depiction of the Vietnam War. A commanding officer, portrayed by Robert Duvall, is standing in the jungle, naked to the waist as American jet fighters roar past overhead. It's morning and already steaming hot. "I love the smell of napalm in the morning," he announces, inhaling deeply. "It smells like victory!"

I feel the same way about the word "no." I love the sound of the word "no." To me, it means action; something is happening. "No's" have a way of eventually leading to the word "yes."

Almost everyone hates the word "no." Salespeople, entrepreneurs, children, lovers, inventors, visionaries, all hate the word "no." And yet it's an indisputable fact of business that if you're not hearing the word "no," you're probably not hearing the word "yes" either. Business involves hearing a whole lot more "no's" than "yes's." There are very few organizations that don't operate on this principle. It's obvious. The more "no's" you hear, the more "yes's" are bound to happen.

In sales, if you hear a thousand "no's" you'll probably hear a hundred "yes's," maybe even two or three hundred. But if you aren't hearing any "no's" whatsoever, then you are not about to hear even a few "yes's."

People avoid making sales calls or contacts or phone calls because they're afraid of the word "no." *What if the person says "no?"* they think. When you hear the word "no," remember there is a "yes" just around the corner. When you hear your second "no," the "yes" is even closer. After the third closer still. Love the word "no"; it's the sound of success in motion. When you're not hearing it, you're in deep trouble.

The Cy Young Award is given each year to the best baseball pitcher in both the American and National Leagues. It is a most coveted award. Its winners are a who's who of baseball's greatest pitchers, from Sandy Koufax to Nolan Ryan to Roger Clemens. The list goes on and on.

However, few people realize that this award is named after the man who holds baseball's record for most career defeats. Yes, that's defeats, not victories. Cy Young lost 313 games, more than any major league pitcher in the history of baseball. Why would they name an award after someone who holds the record for the most defeats, you might ask? Wouldn't it be more appropriate to name it after the person who had the most victories? Well, they did. It's the same man.

Did you know that the great homerun king, Babe Ruth, once held the record for the most strikeouts of any major league player during his career?

A friend of mine, who sells life insurance and is consistently the top salesman for his company, once told me, "I probably hear the word "no" twice or three times as much as my co-workers."

Nobody counts the "no's." Nobody cares about the defeats. The only thing that counts is the victories, the successes—that's what matters.

The next time you feel dejected because someone says "no," remember, "no's" are just the path, the stepping stones leading you to the "yes's."

Persistence

*I've always had sympathy for a guy with an
idea or two who doesn't take no for an answer.*

—MICHAEL BLOOMBERG

I have often thought that there should be a business hall of
fame. A place where the application of great business principles could be honored along with the men and women who
had mastered them successfully, so that we could all admire
their victories and achievements. If there were such a place, the
following story would surely be included under the principle of
"persistence."

Jerry Perenchio was an enterprising entertainment agent
who correctly recognized that promoting the first Ali-Frazier
title match could generate enormous profits.

A little history is necessary at this point. Muhammad Ali was
stripped of his heavyweight title because of his opposition to
the Vietnam War. Undefeated at the time, he was refused a
license to fight for three-and-a-half years. During that time,
there were run-off matches to decide a new champion. Joe
Frazier, a brilliant young fighter with a devastating left hook,
won it all and then successfully defended his championship a
number of times, while Ali fought his battles in the law courts.
Finally, Ali was allowed to fight again.

Two heavyweight champions, both claiming the crown. Both

rightful heirs. Both undefeated. It was a promoter's dream and Jerry Perenchio lay awake at night thinking about how he would market it to the public, to the networks, and sell foreign rights. He knew he could do it. There was a fortune to be made. However, there was one small problem . . . he needed $10 million to pull it off. Where do you get that much money? He was awake one evening thinking about it when he realized he'd have to go out and sell the idea to someone who could put up that kind of money. But who? He made a list of 100 wealthy individuals who could bankroll the project, and he began approaching them one by one.

Now it isn't always easy to get to see powerful and influential people. They are usually well guarded by associates and secretaries, but the power of persistence paid off, and Jerry got to see the first man on the list. It was a very short interview and the man said "no." The second person he approached also said "no." The third person said the same thing. Everyone he approached refused. How discouraging. How many times would thoughts of giving up cross your mind under these circumstances? Not once did they cross Jerry Perenchio's mind. He was determined to promote the fight. He kept working his way through his list.

The twenty-sixth person he approached was Jack Kent Cooke, the owner of the Los Angeles Kings and Lakers. Sitting in Mr. Cooke's office, Jerry presented his plan with the same enthusiasm with which he first conceived his idea. He spoke of the potential for making huge profits, how he would carry out his plan, how everyone would reap the rewards if a $10 million line of credit were put in his hands.

Jack Kent Cooke listened attentively to the young man standing before him. He studied Perenchio's face as the promoter quoted figures and projections, and he made his decision. The answer was "yes."

The rest is history. The Ali-Frazier match was billed as the fight of the century, and through the marketing wizardry of Jerry Perenchio, which was later copied by future promoters, it was the most profitable fight of all time. Everyone made their millions—Ali, Frazier, Jerry Perenchio and Jack Kent Cooke. And the public was rewarded with perhaps the greatest fight ever seen, as Ali lost one of his few professional bouts.

A few months after the event, a journalist asked Jerry Perenchio what he would have done if Jack Kent Cooke hadn't put up the money. The young promoter replied without hesitation, "I would have gone to number twenty-seven."

John Fram, a fast-talking executive with a resemblance to Groucho Marx, also knows well the power of persistence. In 1991 he was an employee of Financial News Network (FNN) when on a hunch he called Michael Bloomberg, founder and CEO of one of the largest media information businesses, with a radical idea. Why not buy FNN and let him run it? "What a dumb idea," Bloomberg responded, cutting John off.

"Look, just give me five minutes in your office," Fram persisted. "I can show you a great opportunity."

Fram got his five minutes, but it didn't help. After a "courtesy listen," he was shown the door. "A total waste of my time," Bloomberg was later to comment.

But it didn't stop John. The next day he called again. "Instead of buying the network, you could develop in-house audio and video programming," he suggested to Bloomberg, changing his pitch somewhat. Once again Bloomberg declined and hung up the phone.

By now you would think Fram would get the message. It was

obvious that Bloomberg wasn't interested. But desire, vision and persistence can make every rejection seem like nothing more than a temporary obstacle to be surmounted. A few days later John called again. This time he shared a whole bunch of new reasons why the financial markets were made for TV. He was eloquent, enthusiastic and fired with vision as he shared his plan.

Bloomberg listened again, and something within him changed. This man who would not take no for an answer was suddenly making sense. Bloomberg hired him on the spot, and so began a business venture that would make them both wealthy. Notice closely the persistence that was necessary to convince Michael Bloomberg of the merits of the project. Most people would have given up after the first rejection. But not John Fram, for he knew clearly what he wanted and was not prepared to accept no for an answer. He was following the old maxim, "The sale begins when the customer says no."

Persistence is one of the ingredients that is absolutely necessary in order to succeed. What magic, mysterious, almost supernatural quality is there in persistence that makes it so effective? It's hard to tell, but we can say with certainty that those who possess this quality almost always succeed.

When Someone Doublecrosses You

*Let us not look back in anger, nor forward in
fear, but around in awareness.* —JAMES THURBER

What do you do when someone doublecrosses you?
Nothing. That's right. Absolutely nothing. Just forget about it and move on. You can't afford to let it
sidetrack you.

The law of averages says that you're going to be cheated
sometimes. Retail stores lose about 3 percent of their revenue
yearly to shoplifters. Storeowners treat this loss as a part of
doing business. They take precautions and prosecute when they
can, but they still lose 3 percent. The important thing is,
however, they don't carry around emotional baggage from
every single incident. The loss is taken in stride.

How many times have you seen people completely destroy
themselves with thoughts of hatred and revenge? Have you ever
seen hate and revenge work positively for someone? Why
would you ever want it in you?

Sometimes it can be someone who is very close to you who
cheats you, and that's hard. Sometimes it is someone you hardly
know. In this world, not everyone operates with honesty and
the highest integrity. This is unfortunate but a fact. Do whatever you can legally if this is an option, but then let go of it.

I know it's hard to do when you are the one who gets cheated, but believe me, the best and shrewdest move you can make is just to forget it and move on. The sooner you do, the sooner you can be back on track, with no heavy baggage to slow you down. Remember, your success and happiness depend upon it.

Names

*We should all be aware of the magic
contained in a name.* —DALE CARNEGIE

Most people don't remember names for the simple reason that they don't take the time and energy necessary to commit those names to memory. They make excuses for themselves; mostly they claim to be too busy to be able to remember them. Or they dismiss the matter by saying, "I can never remember names." No? Well maybe they should. Perhaps they are unaware that to not remember a person's name is sending a message to that person, no matter how subtly, and it's not the type of message you want to be sending.

Conversely, every time you remember a person's name you are saying, "You are important to me." Isn't that valuable?

Franklin D. Roosevelt knew that one of the simplest, most obvious ways of gaining goodwill was by remembering names and making people feel special. The stories are legendary about how the former president of the United States not only remembered the names of people he had met only once, but also those of their wives, and sometimes even their children as well. He took the time to do it because he felt it was important. Besides, being a people-oriented president, he was a smart and savvy politician who knew all the tricks. In fact, he was the only U.S. president to serve three terms consecutively. They passed a law prohibiting it or he might have served four.

The ability to remember names is just as necessary in business and social settings as it is in politics, and its effect is equally powerful.

This being the case, it pays to take the time to remember. Before you begin each day's appointments imagine all the people you are likely to meet. Picture their faces. Then, match names to these faces. The few minutes you spend doing this will be more than compensated by the appreciation you receive from those you greet.

I don't remember names naturally. I have to work at it and I do work at it. Whenever I know I will be attending a business or social gathering where there will be a lot of people, I take five or ten minutes to imagine myself meeting with the people I soon will be seeing, calling them by their names and introducing them to other people. I mentally practice matching the names with the faces. It takes such a little amount of effort and yet it ensures I'll remember everyone's name.

Here's a valuable tip: if you have contact with clients or customers more than once, have their names written on a card filed with their title, along with any other pertinent and valuable information. Add the names of their secretary and receptionist underneath—anybody with whom you have contact. Then, before you go back to see them, you can refer to your card and have their names at your fingertips.

One top-performing executive I know who uses this system also likes to include their hobbies and likes and dislikes. Things like, "son in little league," "wife likes antique furniture," "a Chicago Cubs fan." Then, when he's speaking to these clients after not seeing them for six months or more, he amazes them with this information. Does it impress them? What do you think?

This policy of remembering and honoring the names of friends and business associates was one of the secrets of Andrew Carnegie's stupendous success: it helped him to build a huge steel conglomerate at the turn of this century, and to amass a personal fortune of more than $400 million. At the time, he was the richest man in America. Remembering names was a skill to which he devoted valuable time and energy. He knew and understood the power available to those who master this simple courtesy, and he used it extensively and lavishly.

Another Carnegie, Dale (no relation to above), in his classic book *How to Win Friends and Influence People*, had this to say about the power of a name: "Realize that this single item is wholly and completely owned by the person with whom we are dealing and nobody else. The name sets the individual apart; it makes him or her unique among all others. The information we are imparting or the request we are making takes on a special importance when we approach the situation with the name of the individual. From the waitress to the senior executive, the name will work magic as we deal with others."

New Contacts

Anybody who thinks customers aren't important should try doing without them for ninety days.
　　　　　　　　　　　　　　—BILL BYRNE

It is smart business strategy to stay in touch with as large a circle of contacts as possible. "But I don't have the time, I'm so busy," people lament. All I can say to that is, if you truly want to be successful, you make the time.

Let me introduce you to two individuals who have their own particular methods for staying in touch that work like magic for them. Take what you can from each of these methods, adding or deleting according to your own requirements, and design your own system for staying in contact.

THE TWO-MINUTE PHONE CALL

Daryl Carter works as a salesman for a hardware wholesaler. It's a competitive business with lots of rival firms vying for the retailers' attention. But Daryl has discovered a unique system that keeps him ahead of the pack. He calls it his two-minute phone call. Every working day between 9:30 and 10:30 a.m. he "works the phone," as he lovingly refers to it, making contact with as many people as possible. "I never sell during this period," he says. "If people want to buy or talk longer, I tell them I'll call them back at eleven or two or whatever. I have my daily calendar in front of me at all times and I'm making notes about everything that's said. All I want to do is make contact and let them know I'm thinking about them."

I was intrigued by his method, so I asked Daryl if I could watch him work one morning. He agreed. The next week on the appointed day I met him at his office and he had me sit at a desk opposite his with an extension phone so I could hear the conversations. It was quite revealing. Every call began the same way, with him identifying himself and stating he had only a couple of minutes to spare.

Sometimes he asked questions: "Did you get this order?" "Is everything okay?" "Anything more I can do for you?" Sometimes he informed them of upcoming events: "We've got some really good new products coming up. I'll let you know about them next month." Other times, he just chatted: "How're the kids?" "How's your baseball team doing?" "Have you finished your basement?" "How did your Rotary meeting go?" Sometimes he introduced himself to new businesses. "I know you're happy with the outfit you're dealing with now, but I'm just calling to say I'd love to have your business and we will look after you well if you ever decide to change."

Actually some of his calls lasted three to four minutes. Some less than a minute. But, on average, it was two minutes for each call and, sure enough, personal. Every call was concise and to the point. Nobody complained. Nobody was offended that it was a short call. And almost every one of them (28 out of 30 to be exact) said, "Thanks for calling." They appreciated the contact. "People are busy," says Daryl. "They're happy that you respect their time. They just like to know that you're interested and concerned about them."

And he does this every working day. That's 150 personal

contacts a week. And the next week another 150; 600 calls a month. Month after month after month.

Daryl Carter sells more than four times the next best salesman in the company. Any ideas why?

THE CARDS NEVER STOP

Joe Girard is called the world's greatest salesman. He's even listed in the *Guinness Book of World Records* for his selling feats. The guy's amazing. He sold more cars in his fifteen-year period at a General Motors dealership than any person alive. He would sell more cars in his average day than most good salesmen would sell in a week. On some days he would sell more cars in a day than other salesmen would in a month.

How did he do it? Joe's got great people skills, but you can't sell anything until you have a customer in front of you, and that's where Joe truly shines. He knows that word of mouth is the best way to build a business, so he designed a letter-writing program to make sure his customers would never forget him. Each month, every one of his customers received a card from Joe. In January it was "Happy New Year from Joe Girard," in February it was "Happy Valentine's," in March it was "Happy St. Patrick's Day," and so on, straight through to Thanksgiving and Christmas.

"They loved those cards," said Joe, with a big grin on his face. "Twelve times a year my name appeared in my customers' homes in a very pleasant way. Towards the end of my career I was sending out 14,000 cards a month. I was spending more on stamps than the average car salesman makes in a year." Was it worth it? You bet. Over his career Joe sold more than six cars a day in an industry where the average is one or two a week.

Somebody once said, "When you buy a car from Joe Girard,

you have to leave the country to get away from the guy." Joe took it as a compliment. It was.

Let me share with you an experience of mine. Many years ago I co-founded an entertainment agency, booking groups into lounges and clubs across the country. My partner and I found that everything worked fine as long as one of us spent at least one week a month on the road, making new contacts.

There was only one problem; neither one of us liked to go on the road. So we procrastinated, made up excuses to put off traveling, tried different methods and ignored the obvious fact that when we didn't do it, we were neglecting an important element to the success of our business. Time and again we would build up the business only to watch it slide because we were not going on the road regularly.

Finally, we woke up to the ridiculous situation we were putting ourselves through and solved the problem by hiring someone to work full time on the road. Business boomed.

Looking after business means making new contacts and staying in touch with your old ones. Make sure you are not just paying lip service to this idea. Have a system in place that regularly produces new clients and customers for you and acknowledges the ones you already have, making them feel appreciated. When a company or individual spends at least 10 percent of their working time following this philosophy, they have a solid footing for sustained growth.

Making People Feel Important

Every man I meet is my superior in some way,
in that I learn from him and respect him.

—EMERSON

John Dewey, one of America's most profound philosophers, said that the desire to be important is one of the deepest urges in human nature. William James echoed the same sentiment when he said, "The deepest principle in human nature is the craving to be appreciated." Look around you and see if it isn't so. We all need to be appreciated and acknowledged, to know that our contribution, no matter how small, makes a difference. We need this as surely as we need air and water. The person who understands this and who consistently makes people feel important will not only be surrounded by friends and grateful associates, but will literally write his ticket to wherever he wants to go. It's that important.

I discovered this first-hand working at a summer job between semesters at school. I was a delivery driver for a pharmaceutical company and had about fifty regular customers. One day I printed up a flyer I had written called, "You are a great and marvelous creation." It began, "You are special, you are unique, you can do anything," and went on to complete a short, inspirational message to make people feel good about themselves.

With my own money I printed it up and distributed it to all my customers. Little did I realize the effect it would have.

It empowered everyone I gave it to. It put smiles on their faces, and many of my customers immediately put it up on their walls so they and their customers could see it every day. But it didn't stop there. Two days later I was called into the personnel manager's office. He was beaming. "What did you do?" he asked. "We're getting all these phone calls thanking us for the pamphlet." He asked to see it, and just shook his head in amazement that a delivery driver would take the time and trouble to do such a thing.

A week later, I was brought before the president of the company and introduced as "the man who wrote the pamphlet." The president stood up, shook my hand and, in front of my supervisors, praised me lavishly. You'd think I'd discovered insulin the way he was going on. He asked if he could reprint it and distribute it through the other drivers as well. I happily obliged. Suddenly I was a "star" in the company. Everybody stopped to shake my hand. Salesmen I didn't even know would stop me and say, "You're the one who wrote that pamphlet," and each shared a story about what an impact it had made on one or more of their customers.

I had unwittingly struck a vein of gold, and when I left that job they had a goodbye party for me, and everyone, from the president on down, was there. All this for a part-time summer driver who had worked there for only three months. It taught me a valuable lesson I have never forgotten: "Make people feel important and doors will open."

"The dignity and worth of the individual is a very important part of the HP way," says Bill Hewlett, co-founder of the billion-dollar company, Hewlett Packard. The HP way? That's what they call it, and its people-oriented philosophy has made Hewlett Packard one of the most successfully run companies in America. "I believe that men and women want to do a good job," Hewlett continues, "a creative job, and will do so if they are provided with the proper environment to do so. We treat every employee, no matter what position, with respect, and we recognize personal achievements wherever we find them." And they go out of their way to find them too!

Their corporate objectives, written in a statement of corporate philosophy, begin with: "The achievements of an organization are the result of the combined efforts of each individual."

Smart companies know and understand this. It's good business to make people feel important. Employees are called "crew members" rather than personnel at McDonald's, "hosts" at Disney Productions and "associates" at J.C. Penney. It makes their people feel that they matter, that they belong and are more than just meaningless cogs in a giant wheel. We all need to know this.

Boeing, the most successful airplane manufacturer in the world—with 1997 sales topping $34 billion (US), knows the wisdom of this philosophy. Every time a new plane is ready there is a big celebration in which everyone participates. The plane is rolled onto the tarmac and receptionists, secretaries, maintenance men, engineers, vice-presidents, all gather together. There are toasts and accolades, and everyone is made to feel that they have contributed to make this happen. And, indeed, they have. But what's important is that Boeing actually takes the time and effort to reinforce this for them. They want their employees to feel important, needed and appreciated. So they take the time to do it.

Try it yourself. As an experiment, spend one week making

everyone you meet feel important. Your clients, customers, fellow workers, wife or husband, the taxi driver—look for opportunities to make people feel special, needed and important. At first, it might seem awkward, but you'll soon get the feel of it and actually start enjoying it. Watch how people respond. Keep it up for one full week and watch what happens both to you and those around you. It will be a startling revelation. It will probably change forever the way you deal with people.

Often when people are made to feel important, talents they never even knew they possessed are unleashed. Stevie Morris is an example. Stevie was a withdrawn, introverted young boy in whom self-confidence was sorely lacking. It certainly didn't help that he was blind as well. However, he overcame his handicap as a result of a single incident that changed his life forever.

One day at school, his teacher called upon him to help her with a problem. There was a mouse in the classroom, and after many futile attempts to find it, she realized that Stevie had something nobody else possessed: a remarkable pair of ears, which seemed to have developed to compensate for his blindness. She pointed this out to him and encouraged him to use his extraordinary hearing ability. At first he was shy, but then he reluctantly agreed, and soon they captured the mouse. This was the first time in his life that Stevie's blindness proved to be an asset. Everyone congratulated and praised him. For the first time in his life, Stevie felt important.

Now, many years later, he says that this act of acknowledgement and appreciation was the beginning of a new life for him. From that point on he became determined to develop his gift of hearing, and use it as an asset. And he certainly did. He went on to become one of the great singer-songwriters of his time. His name: Stevie Wonder.

Appreciate people. Encourage them. Acknowledge them. Admire them for qualities or talents they possess. Does it mean anything? You bet.

Nothing is more powerful than positive reinforcement. I have never seen a person, however great or exalted his or her station might be, who did not do better work and put forth a greater effort under the spirit of approval.

How do you make people feel important? Begin by seeing them as important. Start seeing them as a vital part of the whole mechanism. Everyone counts, from your star salesman to the receptionist. Let them know this. With your words, actions, compliments, gifts and cards, there are hundreds of ways to let people know they matter.

Don King has his own special way. Often recognized by the hair that stands straight up on his head, like it's been zapped with an electric current, the infamous fight promoter for Mike Tyson and many of the top heavyweights of the last two decades knows how to make people feel important. Everyone who has ever been greeted by him or who has spent time in his presence experiences this.

"Nobody could make you feel as welcome as Don King," said writer Norman Mailer, recalling his first encounter with him in Zaire. "I'd heard of his reputation, all the stories, but when he greeted you he exuded joy. He made you feel so good." Was it an act? "I don't think so," said fellow writer George Plimpton." He genuinely likes people. He's one of the most charismatic people I've ever met."

Never miss a chance to empower people. The benefits last far beyond the time it takes, and the effects can last for years, even a lifetime. All it takes is a little effort, and the awareness that feeling important is a vital need in us all, a need that goes largely unfulfilled. Fill that need and not only will you feel good, but benefits will flow to you in incredible abundance, and you will be welcomed everywhere you go.

Impressions Count

You only have one opportunity to make a first impression. —UNKNOWN

People judge you by what they know and what they see. And if they don't know you, they judge you only by what they see. Can you blame them?

Always put your best foot forward and present yourself in the best possible way.

Sometimes people think that making an impression is putting on a pretense, that it's false. Not at all. If you are proud of what you do, you owe it to yourself and/or your company to present yourself and your product or service in the best possible light.

We have, of course, all heard stories of individuals who have achieved success while dressing slovenly, being obnoxious, breaking all the rules, and yes, sometimes this happens. But how many others have failed for these very reasons, even though they had something valuable to offer. Countless numbers, let me assure you.

Aristotle Onassis was once asked the secret to his success. "Get a good address," he replied, going on to share how when he first started doing business in America he opened an office on 5th Avenue. "It was only a broom closet," he laughed, "but hardly anyone came there anyway and the letterhead said 5th Avenue, New York; that's what counted."

Media tycoon Michael Bloomburg has similar sentiments. "We always try to have the best office in the most prestigious part of the city," he says from his luxurious Park Avenue headquarters. "When you come to our offices there will be art on the wall, plush carpets, expensive furniture. Aesthetics are important."

Now this is not to say that this should be everybody's style. You can be successful without spending a bundle on accessories, but you can't be successful without impressing people.

How many contracts have been won by a stunning presentation that wowed the participants? A whole lot more than have been won by a mediocre one. When you're trying to sell a product, convince someone of your point of view, or get a promotion, don't be afraid of pulling out all the stops and being at your absolute best. Be afraid of not doing that.

Your office, your business card, your clothes, your manner, your attitude, your style—it all counts. And don't make the foolish mistake of thinking your product or service will, in and of itself, close the deal.

Impressions count, like it or not, so start impressing.

Taking a Good Punch

A champion has to be able to take a good punch. —MUHAMMAD ALI

Muhammad Ali was a boyhood hero of mine. One time when he was in Toronto to fight George Chuvalo (the Canadian Heavyweight), a few of my friends and I skipped school to watch him train in his gym. It was thrilling to watch Ali in action, working the heavy bag and boxing with his sparring partners.

Perhaps he could see the awe in our faces, or maybe he just felt paternalistic, but he decided to pass on some words of wisdom to the admiring crowd. "A champion has got to be able to take a good punch," he admonished, pointing to his chin. "A lot of fighters can throw good punches, but a champion has got to be able to take a good punch and then another good punch and still keep on going."

In your pursuit of success and wealth there will be hundreds, if not thousands of setbacks, disappointments and difficulties. Some will be minor, almost inconsequential. Others will be major crises that necessitate drawing upon all the courage, insight and determination that you can possibly muster. During these times, always keep an overview of the situation. Remember that a heavyweight match is fifteen rounds. If you lose a few rounds, or even get knocked down, it doesn't matter as long as you get back up and eventually win.

I know a clothing manufacturer who worked hard to build up her business. After nearly five years of struggling, she had a big break when a large retailer began carrying her line. She was ecstatic. They eventually became her best customer and accounted for over 50 percent of her business. Everything looked great until one day, without any prior warning, that retailer went into bankruptcy. My friend was left with huge bills and suppliers who desperately needed to be paid, but she was unable to collect that which was owed to her.

What did she do? "I cried, I raged, and I went into denial," she said, thinking back to the incident. "It was as if I was swallowed by a black hole. But then I snapped out of it and started scrambling. I called my suppliers, explained what had happened and made new arrangements with them. I took out a second mortgage on my home. I rallied all the forces I could, and it wasn't easy but we survived." She more than just survived. She now heads a multimillion-dollar enterprise that is well respected throughout the industry and continues to grow yearly.

Knockout punches come fast and hard and they come when you least expect them. A professional boxer never expects the punch that floors him. He defends himself in every way, intending to keep it from ever happening, but still the punch somehow gets by his best defense. Likewise in business and life, you're going to get hit with your share, so you had best know how to handle it.

WHAT TO DO WHEN THE KNOCKOUT PUNCH HITS

1. Don't Panic

This is the cardinal rule in all crises. Whether it's a fire, an illness, a career loss or a business failure—keep your wits about you. Don't rush off madly doing the first thing that comes to your mind. Think everything through clearly; weigh your options before you act.

2. Stay with the Boat

It's amazing how boats will continue to float even when seriously damaged or overturned. This is taught in all seamanship courses. Just because the boat is leaking and filling up with water, don't abandon it prematurely. Often it will continue to float, despite the damage, and thus it is safer to stay with the boat. Don't abandon your situation at the first setback. Maybe you can save the boat, and then again maybe you can't, but stay with it long enough to accurately make that assessment. Only after you're 100 percent positive that it is sinking do you leave.

3. Damage Control

Look at your alternatives and calmly go about putting them into place. Take one step at a time. You're not necessarily going to come up with an answer that will solve your entire problem, but you must stop the hemorrhaging. You're buying time.

I was taught this valuable lesson many years ago when I was an ambulance driver in Toronto. We were instructed very clearly: "Don't try and fix them—all we want is that you bring them to us no worse than you find them. Stop the bleeding, secure the fracture, make sure they're breathing and get them to the hospital fast."

That's what damage control is. It's not necessarily coming up with the solution to the problem, but simply making sure the situation isn't getting worse. Hang in there with whatever positive actions you can until other options present themselves. They always do.

4. Stay Positive

Easy to say I know, when all hell is breaking loose around you, but what is the alternative? Despair? Helplessness? You need your mind working for you during these times, more than ever. The human spirit is incredibly resilient.

No matter how horrific your personal or business setback is, when the dust settles there are options. Businesses do weather incredible storms and setbacks. People do recover from major illnesses. Life does go on when a child is permanently injured. There are second, third and fourth careers out there to explore when you lose your job. Stay positive. Get your mind working for you and you will recover.

5. Don't Beat Up on Yourself

What if I had . . .? If only I'd . . .? You'll think of all the things you could have done. Should have done. But that's hindsight; the fact is you didn't and there's nothing you can do to change that. Maybe things would have turned out different, but what is the point of thinking about it? Regrets and beating up on yourself will only sap your energy. Nobody's perfect, and even with the best of intentions mistakes are made. Regroup and use your energy by directing it into positive channels.

6. Hold Council

Who can you talk to? Who might have gone through a similar situation? Get as much advice and information as you can. Often just being with someone who has had a similar problem is helpful. What did they do? How did they handle it? You don't have to act on everything you hear, but the more information you have, the more effective your decisions will be.

7. Recognize That Time Is on Your Side

Time heals all wounds. How damaging will this incident be?

a) One month from now?

b) One year from now?

c) Ten years from now?

d) Twenty-five years from now?

Put it all in perspective. Take a macro-view of the situation. Sure, it's damaging now, but in the overall view of your life how crucial is it?

The ability to consistently rebound from setbacks and disappointments is the mark of a champion. If you develop this trait, you are sure to survive whatever situation you're going through and eventually rebound. Knockout punches happen to all of us; how we handle them is what makes the difference.

If You Don't Know

I use not only the brains I have, but all I can borrow. —WOODROW WILSON

Ever need more information about a project, a service or a market, and you don't know where to get it? Why not pick up the phone and ask someone who might know? You can call a total stranger. And it's unbelievably effective in getting the information you need.

I first watched this technique in action while sitting in the luxurious office of a successful real estate developer. He was contemplating building some retirement homes. We were discussing the possibility, weighing the pros and cons when he suddenly announced, "I think we need some more information."

Without saying another word, he got out the yellow pages, called one of the major insurance companies and asked to speak to one of their agents. Then, from a person he had never met or spoken to before, my friend proceeded to find out how many people live past the age of fifty-five, what percentage reach sixty-five, seventy-five, what percentage are male, and female, and a wealth of other valuable information. It took him less than five minutes and didn't cost a cent. I was impressed.

How did he do it? He operated from a principle that each of

us would be very wise to remember: People are basically friendly and like to be helpful. It's that simple.

We think nothing of stopping a stranger and asking directions when we're lost. So why not in a business context as well? It's the same principle. Make it a game with yourself and have fun playing detective. See how quickly you can find the information you need.

John Gunn, a successful television producer, needed to get press accreditation fast for a film crew he was sending to Stonehenge in England. The normal channels weren't fast enough. "How to get it?" he pondered.

On a hunch he picked up the phone, called United Press International and asked to speak to the managing editor, a man he'd never spoken to before. He explained his situation. The editor wasn't exactly sure but gave him several phone numbers of people who might know. Two phone calls later, John had his information.

You too can use this principle. When you need information, just ask yourself, "Who would know?" Then get on the phone, introduce yourself and explain your situation and what it is you need. It's extraordinary what information you can obtain when you are willing to network with total strangers. And it's reassuring how helpful they are. Not all the time, sometimes you'll be rebuffed, but nine out of ten times people will either give you the information you need or steer you in a direction where you will soon find it. People are accessible.

Think about it. What would you do if someone called you needing information and you could supply it easily and effortlessly, and by doing so it would help this person immeasurably? You would provide the information, and after you hung up the phone you'd feel good about it. We like to be helpful. It makes us feel good.

In our age of information technology you can rapidly access a wealth of information via computers and the Internet. But sometimes the simple telephone and phone book are all you need.

A Pleasing Personality

I know of no more encouraging fact than the
unquestionable ability of man to elevate his
life by conscious endeavor.   —THOREAU

People would rather do business with people they like than those they don't. This is so obvious that it hardly seems to need stating, yet so many of us, when dealing with business associates, customers and clients, simply go through the motions. It becomes almost mechanical. There's no enthusiasm, warmth or rapport. This is unfortunate and damaging.

You might be able to separate yourself from your product or service, but almost everyone else you come in contact with cannot. From another's perspective, you and your product are a package. Like it or not, who you are is either an asset or a liability to your success.

This being said, doesn't it make sense to develop a personality that is pleasing and attractive to other people? I can hear the howls of protest already: "This is who I am"; "People can either accept me or not"; "I can't change"; "I'm not going to be somebody I'm not."

What nonsense. Lighten up. Why not make some changes? Your personality is a creation. You can change any part you don't like. Take Benjamin Franklin as an example. Franklin, one of the founding fathers of the American Confederation, was a man with a brilliant mind. Nobody who had any contact with him doubted this. However, he felt his personality could be worked on, so he resolved to make some changes and, in his autobiography, he shares the methods by which he achieved this.

He made a list of thirteen qualities he wished to adopt. Having made a thorough self-examination, he knew what he needed to develop in himself. "I made a little book, in which I allotted a page for each of the virtues. Then I charted my progress, as it was my intention to acquire the habit of all these virtues."

Realizing he could not attempt to acquire them all at once, he picked one a week and concentrated on living that quality for the full week. The next week he went on to the second quality, until he had worked upon all thirteen. Then he began again. He was able to complete this cycle four times in a year. This practice was so successful that his friends and associates were amazed with the changes.

Benjamin Franklin went on to become one of the most influential men of his time. A creative inventor and brilliant statesman, he was widely respected and admired by his peers. Would he have accomplished all this without having worked on his personality? We will never know, but I somehow doubt it.

Your personality is either attracting or repelling people. When you fully realize this, you will understand the importance of creating a personality that draws people and opportunities to you. A recent study showed that the ten most admired qualities in a person are:

1. Sense of humor
2. Sincerity
3. Honesty
4. Openness and receptiveness

   5. Positive attitude
   6. Compassion
   7. Patience
   8. Good listening ability
   9. Confidence
  10. Politeness

How many of these qualities do you possess? Test yourself. Or better yet, ask someone who knows you well to do an evaluation. Ask for honesty and brace yourself for the result. It's often a sobering realization to find out we're not quite as perfect as we'd like to think.

If you have all ten, you're operating at 100 percent efficiency on the personable scale. But very few people will be at that level. If you find that you have five or fewer of these qualities, then there's work to be done. Let's assume for a moment that you have five. If you add one more quality, you've improved by 20 percent. Add two qualities and you've increased by 40 percent. That's incredible growth. Anybody doing so is sure to notice startling changes in his or her life.

As a child, how you were raised, what you experienced, were often dictated by circumstances—and by others. But, as an adult, your personality and character are under your control and entirely your own responsibility; you can hold no other person responsible for who you are. If there are parts of you that you don't like, why accept them? Resolve to change. If there are qualities you admire in others, make them yours.

Your personality is an evolution of your thoughts and habits. As your thoughts and habits change, so does your personality. How you act today will determine what you will become tomorrow.

It's an exhilarating feeling to realize that it's not a matter of discovering who we are, so much as deciding who we want to be, and then becoming that person. Don't be afraid to change. Change is a part of life. Who you are today is not who you were in the past or will be in the future. Understanding this, why not actively choose your changes and adopt some qualities you've always admired in others?

Honesty

There's no such thing as a minor lapse of integrity.   **—TOM PETERS**

B e scrupulously fair and honest in all your dealings. Even if doing so costs you money, in the long run it always pays off. If you have the opportunity of short-changing someone without them knowing it—don't. Honor your word. Deliver what you promise. Keep your commitments. This is how business relationships are maintained, and how they grow into long-term clients.

There is no pride or inner satisfaction in lying, cheating, or giving less than you promised, no matter what the reward, real or imagined. Short-term gain often leads to long-term shame and, in the final analysis, you must live with your decision. A reputation lost can never be regained, while a reputation enhanced by integrity and honesty will repay you many times over.

I know I differ here from those promoting the "win at all cost" philosophy, but true success means more than an accumulation of dollars and cents. The dignity and honor that comes with honesty is an asset to oneself that's truly invaluable. Operate at the highest ethical and moral standards and people will respond to this; they will respect you for it. It's not just good manners, it's smart business.

Good people regularly and consistently finish first, and don't let anyone tell you differently. Not only do they finish first, but they have fuller, richer and happier lives.

Remember, we go this way but once. Enjoy the treasures and joys that life affords you, but most importantly, make the journey an honorable one. In the end, there's no doubt you'll be glad you did.

Listening

When two people understand each other in
their innermost hearts, their words are sweet
and strong, like the fragrance of orchids.

—I CHING

Most of us are actually very poor listeners. Does this surprise you? It probably does, since most of us think of ourselves as open, receptive and responsive to others. Why would we not listen to someone when it is in our best interest to understand fully what people think and feel? We don't do it intentionally; we do it unconsciously. We do it because we aren't aware of how our mind censors and filters out information.

We walk around as if we're receptive, but often we're so filled with our own opinions, judgments and know-how that nothing new can enter. When you really listen, you create a space within yourself to learn and accept and discover from others. It's so rewarding. What's more, people will experience you listening to them and they will appreciate it and respond accordingly.

The first step in developing improved listening skills is to understand how our mind both interprets and ignores certain signals. We filter everything through our personal lens of reality. We try to figure people out, to explain their motives, their behavior, based on our own values and experiences. What a mistake. We respond to what we think we should be hearing from them, rather than what we are actually hearing. We find ourselves superimposing our reality onto others without even realizing we're doing it.

A colleague at work comes to you with a personal problem. You begin listening, but very quickly you are not only listening, you're using your mind to try to solve the problem. You feel the need to be efficient and helpful, so you're looking for solutions even while he's still talking. Your mind jumps between listening, judging, analyzing and projecting solutions, and the more your analytic mind processes these options, the less you hear. We all do this.

We find ourselves primarily in our own thoughts, not with those of the other person. Rather than experience their reality as direct, fresh, authentic, complete, and within their own values, fears, knowledge and confusion, we make a quick and erroneous leap into an interpretation distorted by the lens of who we are. Not only are we listening less, but our mind begins to act as a screen that preselects information, deciding which is valuable, which is not.

The result of all this mental activity is that there is less room to meet, less space for a new truth to emerge, less possibility to let things simply be revealed. And we misunderstand what the person is trying to share with us.

Your ability to listen well and receive clearly the information that is being transmitted to you from another individual is essential if you wish to communicate deeply and effectively. Whether you're a manager, a parent, a spouse or a salesperson, your ability to understand what is happening within another individual and respond appropriately is determined by how well you can listen and truly hear what is being said.

HOW TO BE A GOOD LISTENER

1. *Listen with the intention to deeply understand.*

Practice listening carefully, intently, missing nothing. Stephen Covey, author of *The 7 Habits of Highly Effective People*, states, "Seek first to understand, then to be understood. Listen with the intention to deeply understand." Most people do not listen with the intent to understand; they listen with the intent to reply. Salespeople often make this mistake in their eagerness to make the sale.

Let me introduce you to a super listener, and a super salesman, Joe Gandolfo. Joe sells more life insurance than any other person in the world. Forget a million dollars a year—one year Joe sold a billion dollars' worth. Yes, that's one *billion*. With those credentials, he deserves to be heard. "Salespeople's biggest problem is that they do too much talking and not enough listening," he says. "I believe that a good rule for a salesperson to follow is to count to five after the prospect has finished speaking before you say anything. This way you are sure there's nothing more he wants to say. That's important."

When your client or customer is speaking, they are sharing with you what they want, what they don't want, how they feel. They're giving you their perspective. Isn't that valuable? Too often, all this is missed in the rush to make the sale. Sometimes your position and presentation are prepared even before you walk in the door. And when your customer speaks, you are only paying lip service to what they say, all the while watching for openings to jump in and get your selling points across. And that's the problem. We think we already know what they're going to say. We think we know what they want.

Take a lesson from John F. McDonnell, past CEO of McDonnell Douglas, who learned this principle the hard way. "We did not always listen to what the customers had to say before telling them what they wanted."

All that changed quickly when McDonnell Douglas noticed their market share slipping drastically. The engineers and company representatives soon took to regularly working with their clients on their own turf, learning all they could about their customers' needs. "We learned to do a lot of listening," said McDonnell.

2. Listen with your heart and not just your mind.

The essence of authentic listening is not that you agree with someone or come up with brilliant solutions; it's that you fully understand what that person is going through emotionally as well as intellectually. You live it with them, through their eyes and values. You listen to not just what is said, but what is not said. You listen for feeling, emotion. You sense, you intuit, you feel for meaning beyond the words. You listen with all your senses. Only a small part of what is being communicated to you is coming through the words. Be receptive to all the signals and messages coming through both consciously and subconsciously. Trust your instinct and what you feel. Listen with all your senses.

Greg Singer runs a successful wholesale food company. He told me about how, one day, one of his biggest customers balked at a price increase for one of Greg's products. "I knew that this buyer was under pressure to cut costs," he shared with me, "but on that particular product, our profit was negligible and we were long overdue for a price increase, so I refused to budge. I held my position and I was right to do so. But what I didn't do was see the overall situation of what he needed and wanted. I got stuck on a point of principle. Instead of giving in and maybe even losing a little on that product, I held my ground with my arguments and logic on why I had to raise the price. He reluctantly agreed, but instinctively I knew he resented it. A few months later I lost the whole account and I'm sure it stemmed from that incident. Now, I always put myself in the customer's position and look closely at the whole situation before I say or do anything. I don't ever want to lose another account by being short-sighted."

3. *Practice stopping the mind from judging and projecting.* Watch yourself. Watch how you turn off, project, come up with resolutions, all while the person is still talking. Catch yourself doing it. Being aware that you do this is the first step in eliminating it. Authentic listening cannot be done at the same time as thinking, so practice letting go and just listening. Be with the other person one hundred percent; never mind solutions and answers; they will come naturally. Just hear and listen with all your senses.

When our awareness remains quiet and clear, there's depth to our perspective. In the clarity of a mind that is authentically listening, there is room for us to see and hear whatever is actually happening, and whatever might be left unsaid. Though our mind hears many details, our attention becomes a heart-to-heart experience and is felt deeply. In moments like these we feel our connectedness, and the inherent potential of how we can help one another. Solutions and insights make themselves known. We don't have to figure them out; they come by themselves, with greater wisdom than we could ever imagine.

We need to hear and understand what others are sharing with

us, and to be open to changing the way we listen. We need to include other important aspects of communication that we've maybe ignored. The first step is to realize how much we're missing with our old habits.

Let me share a story with you. It happened to a colleague of mine after we spent a very stimulating evening discussing the principle of listening and how often we don't really hear what people are saying to us. The next morning, we were to get together again for an early meeting. He got up at 6:30 a.m. and was eating breakfast when his young daughter came to join him. His wife was still asleep. After a minute or so, his little girl looked up at him and said, "Daddy, I love you." He was momentarily taken aback, and, overcome with emotion, he asked her, "Why did you say that?" "Daddy!" she replied, "I say that to you every morning."

"I never knew that, or had never really heard it before," he shared with me. We both just sat there and looked at one another in stunned silence. How much are we missing?

Role Models

*Our chief want is somebody who will make us
do what we can.* —EMERSON

The honoring of heroes shouldn't disappear with adolescence. Heroes can and should be a lifelong source of inspiration and motivation for us. Many of the most famous and influential people we know let great men and women shape their lives well into their own adulthood, and so can you.

Long before he ever became a Beatle, John Lennon idolized many of the old rhythm and blues greats, people like Chuck Berry and Muddy Waters. He had their pictures on his wall and used them as inspiration when he first began playing guitar. In this way he could imagine that he was them. This process is not just idle daydreaming; it allows new creative ideas to be released from the subconscious. It allows us to move beyond our preconceived limitations. It is an excellent process for developing inspiration and creativity.

Woody Allen watched the Marx Brothers' films hundreds of times and dreamed of being just as funny and talented. It's no secret that Groucho Marx was a major influence on the talented filmmaker.

Billionaire Ted Turner studied the Greek classics in university.

His father, a very practical businessman, couldn't understand why his son was wasting his time with these studies. What he didn't realize was that Ted was conditioning his mind with images of the fabled Greek heroes who seized opportunities, turned sure defeats into victories, and surmounted innumerable obstacles in order to achieve their goals. Much the same as Ted would do in his later life.

Singer Whitney Houston watched her older cousin Dionne Warwick release hit after hit and dreamed of one day being just like her. She was fortunate in that she had a family member to model herself after as she worked her way toward eventual superstardom. She could go into the recording studios, see Dionne perform live, watch how she handled different situations. All this had a tremendous impact on Ms. Houston, but you don't have to actually know the person in order to model yourself after him or her. Nor do you even have to meet that person. Few of us get that chance, yet we can still use inspirational individuals as our role models.

A millionaire clothing manufacturer once shared with me how in her early years, while struggling to succeed, she would draw inspiration from other successful women. She had pictures on her wall of prominent women who had made it. They became her mentors. Each time she looked at the pictures it gave her encouragement. If they could do it, she could too, she reminded herself. And she did.

All big companies that pride themselves on excellence have what are called their "war stories." IBM, Microsoft, 3M, and Hewlett Packard, all have them; stories of past employees who performed great feats under difficult circumstances. These were people who achieved spectacular results, men and women who did the impossible, who surmounted all odds and won.

They became part of the companies' lore, like folk legends, and today continue to inspire others to carry on in the same tradition.

We all need to know that what we're trying to accomplish can in fact be achieved. Perhaps it will take an almost superhuman effort, but we have to believe that if we harness all our resources and determination, it can be done. And this is what our heroes can do for us—they can prove to us that our goals are not impossible.

They can also show us *how* to proceed in any given situation, especially a difficult one. In *Mind Power Into the 21st Century* I mention the example of Napoleon Hill, millionaire author of *Think and Grow Rich*, who regularly convened, in his mind, his "invisible counselors." He chose nine men whose lives and life works had been most impressive to him. Just before going to sleep at night he would close his eyes and imagine this group of men seated with him around his council table. He would discuss what projects he was working on and ask for assistance. Although he is emphatic that these sessions occurred entirely in his imagination, he is equally adamant that the ideas generated through this process led him "into glorious paths of adventure and wealth." He was so impressed with the results that he made these inner sessions a daily habit.

Such contemporaries as first lady Hillary Clinton and TV host Larry King have used similar methods to have imaginary conversations and seek advice from those they respect and admire. Most people assume that this occurs only in the imagination, but is it only that? There are some who feel the past, present and future are all contained within the moment. Nobel-winning physicist David Bohm, a protégé of Einstein's and one of the world's most respected quantum physicists, sees the world as holographic and always existing within the present. If this model of reality is true, then having a "real" conversation or connecting with another individual in the past or future would theoretically be entirely possible.

Because it defies our logic does not mean it can't be done. Nineteen-year-old Graham Kearney certainly believes it can. An artist with prodigious talent, Graham started painting at the age of five. He had his first show in 1994 when he was fourteen, and he received immediate acclaim. Soon after he began receiving commissions, and his paintings now grace the lobbies of major hotels and the homes of wealthy patrons around the world. While he was honing his painting skills, Graham would imagine himself having conversations with the great artists of the past. "It was as if they were really with me," he insists. "It was more than just my imagination. I really felt their presence guiding me." Was this gifted young man actually instructed by the great masters? Can we also do the same? Or was it simply the subconscious responding in an extraordinary fashion to the demands put upon it? Does it matter? We will probably never know for certain, but the process nonetheless is clearly powerful and available to everyone.

When we model ourselves after those who have achieved greatness, we take on their character, their strengths and their determination. Soon their success leads to our success, and in the process we better ourselves.

Role modeling is an effective and powerful step in achieving success, because it supplies us with inspiration and encourages us to move beyond temporary failures. It also stimulates the creative imagination and draws from the subconscious mind ideas and insights that would not come to us unless we were so inspired.

And let us not forget the most important principle of all. Whatever you think about, dwell upon, focus on will make an imprint on the subconscious mind. You can imprint the very qualities you admire in your mentors. This ultimately is the greatest gift they give us. So choose your heroes and role models wisely, and let them lift you to heights you could not hope to accomplish on your own..

PART III

◆ ◆ ◆

BALANCE

Leisure

Better to have loafed and lost, than never to have loafed at all. —JERRY GILLIES

When I am speaking to the assembled executives and employees of a corporation I often startle my audience by suggesting that the key to their success is in working less, not more. And I mean it.

Leisure is just as necessary to success as work. It is the right balance of the two that allows you to perform effectively and consistently. Never forget that.

The most common error in today's typical work habit, as I see it, is not that people aren't working hard enough (they surely are), but that they are not giving themselves enough quality leisure time. And their work is suffering as a result.

Leisure is not a reward for a job well done; leisure is part of the job. This is an important distinction. You don't oil and grease your car at the end of a long journey: you need the oil and grease *during* the journey, so your car will run smoothly.

Leisure allows you to relax, to let go, to give the mind a break. This is necessary, for it is when the mind is in a state of relaxation, away from the quotas and deadlines, that creative ideas are given the opportunity to surface and make themselves known.

Universities have, for centuries, operated with this principle. They call it a sabbatical; faculty members are entitled to a one-semester sabbatical, with pay, every six or seven years. They often extend their sabbaticals by taking a second semester off without pay. They are encouraged to take this time off to study or travel and, most importantly, to escape from the duties of professorship. The theory is that, after the break, the professor will come back invigorated, with new, stimulating ideas that in turn will enrich the university and its students. The theory is well grounded in fact.

Burke Stintson, AT&T's senior public relations manager, believes strongly in the practice. Since 1992 about 1,500 employees have taken sabbaticals at AT&T. "We see it as a way for people to better themselves and bring new skills and perspectives back to our workplace."

At the Segal Company, a consulting firm based in Manhattan, employees get a one-month paid sabbatical after ten years. They get two months after fifteen years and four months after twenty-five years. Segal was one of the first companies to offer sabbaticals, initiating the program in the early 1960s. The time off may be used for any purpose: pursuing a hobby, painting the house, taking a course or traveling. "The Segal Company program was founded with two basic purposes in mind." Says Robert Krinsky, the chairman and administrator of the sabbatical program. "First, a sabbatical should help you gain a new perspective on your work and life, and this is of immense value. Secondly it provides an opportunity for someone else in the firm to take on different responsibilities."

At Genentech, a biotechnology company in south San Francisco, full-time employees, in addition to their regular vacation time, are eligible for a sabbatical of six continuous weeks with full pay. "The sabbatical program is one of several rewards given to employees in acknowledgment of the high level of intensive work and commitment required at Genentech," says Judy Heyboer, the company's president of human resources.

"High level intensive work." Sound familiar? It seems to be the norm in today's working environment, but what about balance?

"Part of having a people-centered company is recognizing that balance is important in everyone's life," says Frank Phillips, who oversees a pension consulting and money management firm in Washington. "We don't celebrate eighty-hour weeks around here. In fact, we think that the person who has to work like that is, in the long run, not very smart."

We have been taught, wrongly, that hard work is the way to success. Hard work without the balance of leisure almost always leads to failure. It is the leisure time between work that allows you to return to your project again and again, refreshed, with renewed vigor and enthusiasm.

Now we can't all take a year's leave from our occupations, so we must be diligent in taking holidays, weekends, plus the occasional day off here and there. It is negligent and foolish to do otherwise.

It is interesting to note that most major achievers in this world have reported that they made their biggest breakthroughs after taking time out for contemplation and reassessment. This is not hard to understand because when you are idle, your subconscious mind (the creative mind) advances full-steam ahead. It's very often during these idle times that brilliant, new ideas come forth. Paul Boyer, 1997 Nobel Laureate, relaxing in his house overlooking L.A., agrees, "Getting away from it all, letting go, is more conducive to innovation than focusing continuously on your project."

Remember, it is the balance of work and leisure that will most surely and directly bring you success. Take time out this evening and think of ten ways that you can include more leisure in your week. What do you enjoy doing? What gives you pleasure? Discipline yourself to include these activities in your daily routine.

And for those of you who foolishly think you can't afford the luxury to take leisure time, I've got a message for you: You can't afford not to. If you want to do quality work consistently, day in and day out, you have to give yourself quality leisure. Anything else is fooling yourself. And it's your work that will suffer as a result.

We have all seen and experienced the burnout that happens with too much work. As the Zen saying goes, "The bow kept forever taut will break." This is a fact that we ignore at our own peril. Give yourself quality time to relax and enjoy leisure activities, not because you're lazy, but because you love success.

Making a Difference

You must be the change you wish to see in the world.
— GANDHI

How do you make a difference? Ironically, you can do it through almost every action you take. You do it when you wipe your child's face, when you cheer up someone who's depressed, when you visit your parents or grandparents, when you congratulate someone on a job well done. One doesn't have to change the world to make a difference; one just has to become more aware and caring.

Fay Stockill makes a difference. She has a self-help program that she takes into the prisons, teaching the inmates self-esteem and positive thinking. "The one thing these people have a lot of," she says, "is time to think." She also realizes that the thoughts they think in prison will undoubtedly determine what happens to them when they're outside again. So she helps. It's a nourishing, enriching, well-thought-out program created by a woman who cares—and the results are spectacular. Several times I've gone to a prison with Fay and watched her work. Fay is a small, somewhat shy woman, the last person you'd expect to be doing this type of work, but she believes passionately in what she is doing. When she talks about the human potential, her eyes light up. The prisoners love her, and the respect is etched on their faces every time she enters the room.

To hear these grown men, some hardened, some bitter, share their most intimate experiences, to see them open up and sometimes cry, is humbling. All the while, Fay is there supporting them, encouraging them, feeding them with positive messages, making them believe in themselves because she believes in them. You would think she would be welcomed with open arms by the prison authorities. She's not. She fights the bureaucracy every inch of the way. First she's being paid, then, after a few months, there is no more money in the budget. It's disheartening. But Fay takes it in stride. She continues in spite of all this because she believes she can make a difference.

Anna Aviles is a music teacher at public school 161 in Brooklyn, New York. Her students are mostly underprivileged kids who don't always believe in themselves. Who can blame them? Their surroundings give them little cause for hope. But Anna believes in her charges, and her goal is to make them feel good about themselves. "If they can feel good about themselves in even one area of their life, then they can feel good about themselves in other areas, too," she states with conviction. "All they need to do is succeed in one area, just one, and that triggers the belief that they can do it in others as well."

So they mount plays together. Ten-year-olds, twelve-year-olds, fourteen-year-olds rehearsing and staging Broadway hits. And when they finish, their play becomes a local community event. In staging these shows, Anna's students begin at 7:30 a.m., one hour before school starts, and they stay after school as well. They learn co-operation, discipline, how to begin and finish a project, how to turn an idea into reality, and they have fun too. When it's all over, they are left with a feeling of accomplishment, and a belief in themselves. They know they have succeeded in this one area of their lives, and they begin to think of the future from a different perspective. Maybe, just maybe, they think, they could do it again. Anna Aviles is making a difference.

Glyn Evans is a partner in Stonehenge Filmworks, a film and video production house in Toronto, Canada. I met him when his company did some promotional work for us several years ago. Glyn belongs to the Big Brothers Association, an international organization helping boys who don't have fathers. Once a week he takes his little "brother" on an outing—to a baseball game, a movie, or just somewhere they can spend time together. They've developed quite a bond. Glyn works long hours. Often he's so busy he doesn't really have the time to go on these outings, but he makes the time. I've seen him leave early from an important meeting to keep an appointment with his little brother. It's a commitment he's made, and he keeps it. Glyn Evans is making a difference.

You can never be too young or too old to make a difference. Each of us has a contribution to make. David Levitt started making a difference in grade six. Noticing all the food that was thrown away in the school cafeteria each day, he wondered, "Wouldn't it be possible to give it away to the homeless?" He convinced his school in Tampa Bay, Florida to do just that. The year was 1994. Four years later, in 1998, "The Harvest Program," as it is now called, has 144 schools all over Florida participating in what was once originally just "one little boy's idea." David Levitt is making a difference.

Ten years ago, our company decided to devote 10 percent of our profits to a Making a Difference Fund, which we created. The money would then be dispersed to groups; individuals and organizations that are making a difference, that are helping to make this world a better place. It's funny; it seemed so revolutionary and radical at the time. Little did I realize what joy, pleasure and satisfaction this decision would bring. We decided right in the beginning to focus on smaller, grass roots organizations that don't get much attention and that really needed our money.

These past ten years we've thrown parties for underprivileged children, sponsored Fay Stockhill in her prison work, helped an unemployment drop-in center, paid the rent for a women's shelter, and given grants to disabled athletes, Greenpeace, youth groups and countless others. It's the most wonderful feeling, and I'm confident that in a small way we are making a difference. And it's only the beginning.

Recently I was watching television; the head of a major multinational company was defending its corporate record to a probing reporter. "We're good corporate citizens," he shot back in response to the suggestion that they might not be doing enough. And it got me thinking—"good corporate citizen," what does that mean? Paying taxes? Grants to charities? Support for the arts? Or is there more? What are the responsibilities of corporations, and individuals for that matter? Can and should we do more for our communities and the world we live in? Anita Roddick has some strong views on this.

Anita is the founder of The Body Shop International. Her story is already a legend in the United Kingdom. A thirty-three-year-old housewife with two young daughters had an idea for a store that would feature natural skin, hair and body care products. With a $7,000 bank loan, she and her husband proceeded to set up shop. Now The Body Shop operates successfully in over forty countries and is a $1 billion plus company. But it's not their growth that is so unusual—it's their attitude. The Body Shop is almost as well known for its passionate environmentalism as for its cosmetics. Roddick has incorporated her environmental beliefs into the business, offering only biodegradable products, for example, and providing refillable containers. The company even has an Environmental Projects department. And it uses its shops as the base for a series of highly visible campaigns to save the whales and stop the destruction of rain forests, among many other worthy causes.

Anita believes that businesses should do more than make money, create decent jobs and sell good products. "Companies should actually help solve our major social problems, not just by contributing a percentage of their profits to charities, but by using their resources to come up with real answers. Business is just another form of human enterprise, so why should we expect and accept less from it than we do from ourselves?" she argues convincingly. And Anita has a vision: "I believe quite passionately that there is a better way. I think we can rewrite the book on business. I believe you can trade ethically, be committed to social causes and empower your employees all at the same time."

I believe that the time will come when corporations will recognize they have a responsibility to make a difference in the world, when they will be inspired by the challenge and embrace it at first slowly, then eagerly, when they will consider profit only one of the measures of success. An important one to be sure, but community responsibility and global solutions will be high on their priority list as well.

It will take people, people who are in responsible positions both in government and business and who are prepared to make courageous decisions and commitments. It will take more people like Fay Stockill, Anna Aviles, David Levitt and Glyn Evans who, despite their busy lives, take the time to make a difference. It will take a change in priorities and values and beliefs in all of us, but it's not impossible. It can happen if we truly want it.

I have taken a positive perspective in all this for a good reason.

I believe the image we hold of the future plays a role in helping that future emerge. The potential strength of our society will be created by the intensity and energy of our images of the future. The future is not fixed. It doesn't just happen. The choice of whether or not we move in this direction rests very much with us. It's our decisions and actions that will ultimately make the difference. We all make choices in our lives. We can choose to make a difference.

Let's begin by being optimistic. "Optimism is a strategy for making a better future," said writer and activist Noam Chomsky, "Because unless you believe that the future can be better, it's unlikely you will step up and take responsibility for making it so. If you assume that there's no hope, you guarantee that there will be no hope. If you assume that there are opportunities to change things, there's a chance you may contribute to making a better world. The choice is yours."

Social activist, and former Secretary of Health and Education in the U.S., John Gardner has said, "People want to work hard on something they believe in. People are basically good and loving and caring, but what's happening is that most of us don't know where to start." How can I as a single individual make a difference, we seem to be saying? The answer is simple—start with the fragment of the universe that is right in front of you.

A woman friend of mine shared with me how, when she goes to the beach, she makes sure she takes away not only her own litter, but a little extra as well. "I don't make a big issue of it," she says. "I don't try and clean the entire beach. But every time I go, I take at least one extra piece of garbage back with me, something I didn't bring. That way I feel the beach is better off for me having been there." That's beautiful. And we can adopt that sentiment in all aspects of our lives. We can all make a difference.

Fun

*In your haste to make a living, don't forget to
make a life.*   —UNKNOWN

Have fun three times every day. Sound too frivolous? Am
I suggesting you not take your work seriously? Not at
all. The mind needs diversification and thrives on
variety. When you can mix fun into your business day, and make
it a habit, your work will always be more effective.

How much time does it take to have fun? Sometimes just a
few moments. You can have fun in almost any situation. When
you are driving to work and enjoying a good song on the
radio—that's fun. A joke shared with a fellow employee, a
chapter read in a good novel, even a brisk walk in the sunshine
or a workout at the gym can be fun.

I shared this principle with an associate of mine who tends
to be very serious. He listened carefully and then decided to
give it a try. I'll let him tell you about what happened:

"I had a few appointments out of the office the day after John
told me about the principle of having fun three times a day. I
was skeptical, but how could I successfully dispute it until I'd at
least tried to do it? I must admit, though, I didn't have a clue
where the fun would come from.

"I was driving along listening to the radio when I passed a

music store. I remembered that there was a CD I wanted to buy. I parked the car, purchased the CD so I could listen to music in the car. This counts as fun I thought, and it was incredibly soothing to listen to the music instead of the incessant chatter of the radio. Good, that's one I thought, warming to the challenge.

"Usually when I'm out on calls I grab a sandwich or burger and eat it on the run. However, today I thought I'd stop and have a sit-down meal. That will be my second bit of fun. I found an Italian restaurant, ordered pasta and even had a glass of wine, something I rarely do at lunch. I was out within forty-five minutes and it felt great to have had that break—it was fun.

"The third bit of fun was the best. As I was approaching the office I had a radical idea. Instead of taking my usual spot, why not park farther away from the office and walk. I love walking—never do enough of it and usually feel guilty about not getting any exercise. So here I was parking ten blocks from my office and walking. It felt so bold, unusual, illogical—I loved it. The ten-block walk took about fifteen minutes. It was a sunny day and I enjoyed it immensely. And I had my fun three times. I hate to admit it but I think he might be onto something here. I'm going to try it again, and you know what? I think I've found a new parking spot."

My friend's awakening to the joy of fun and how easily you can bring it into your life was revolutionary for him. In subsequent talks I watched how he brought this principle into his relationship with his wife and children. His life in general started being more fun.

We must ensure that every day has some fun in it. Make a list of all the activities that can be fun for you and see how many of them you can include in your daily routine. Practice having

spontaneous fun. Look for opportunities to have fun. Be creative and acknowledge yourself for doing it. Remind yourself
you're having fun when it's happening. This increases the
pleasure of fun and makes it more immediate. Sometimes we
get so busy in our minds that we don't even recognize the fun
when it's happening. Don't miss out on your fun while you're
having it.

Fun gives you energy. It empowers you, refreshes you, helps
you work better. So don't deny yourself these benefits. Make
fun an important part of every single day. It is smart, healthy,
empowering, nourishing, productive, beneficial and, oh yes, I
almost forgot the most important part—it's fun.

The View

We live at the edge of the miraculous.
—HENRY MILLER

Several years ago, when I was doing a seminar in Sydney, Australia, one of my course participants asked if I would visit his father, who had recently been diagnosed with cancer. The disease had apparently spread through more than 60 percent of his father's body, and there was essentially no possibility of recovery. The father's doctor had told him he had only three months to live. The family was devastated; the father overcome with shock.

I agreed and a time was set up for me to see him. I took a taxi to his house, and he greeted me at the door. He thanked me for coming. The family had arranged that we be alone for an hour. It is an hour I will never forget.

We talked for fifteen or twenty minutes about life, and its impermanence. He then invited me outside to his backyard: It had a stunning view of the water and the Sydney Opera House, and I could see sailboats gliding throughout the harbor. It was magnificent. And then he said something that shook me to the core. He said, "John, I'm a very practical man with practical ideals. I believe in working hard to support my family and give them a good lifestyle. I guess you could say I'm a workaholic . . .

or was a workaholic," he corrected himself with a thin smile. "I've lived in this house for twenty years. It will be twenty years this September. Four days ago, when I returned from the doctor's office with the news that I had only three months to live, I was crushed. I came out here and sat where we're sitting right now and looked at the view. I looked at how beautiful and serene it was. And I suddenly realized I had never seen the view before. Not really. Oh sure, I had come out here and looked at it hundreds of times, but I was always thinking of my business. There was always something on my mind. I never really just stopped to enjoy it. And it's so beautiful . . ." His voice trailed off and he began to cry. We both just stood there. Two grown men sharing the anguish of the moment.

I wish I could say this story had a happy ending, but it didn't. The father died a few months after I saw him. However, there is a lesson to be learned here. Simply put, it is, "Don't forget the view." And the view is what happens to you each and every day of your life. The view is your life. Don't miss it. Don't let it pass you by. John Lennon said it beautifully: "Life is what happens while we're busy making other plans." And that's what happens. We get busy. We get too busy to appreciate. We also fall into the trap of categorizing every event as good or bad, positive or negative. Things that make us feel good and things that don't. But aren't all experiences a part of life, and why must life always be pleasant?

When we expect life to always feel good, to always please us by bringing us the things we desire, we live an illusion. How pitiful. It's neurotic to need to be happy, fulfilled and stimulated every hour of every day. We've become so miserly. We have left no room for pain, confusion or boredom to enter freely into our life. We shun and reject anything unpleasant. But in fleeing from these experiences, instead of accepting them as a part of our life, we have unconsciously rejected life. We bleed and suffer needlessly over the most inconsequential details. We fail to realize, as a friend of mine likes to say, that "Life is a package deal." You don't get to pick and choose. You don't get to say I like this but I don't like that. It's a package. Take it or leave it. Even failure, sickness and misfortune play their part in the grand scheme of a life unfolding.

Accepting life in its entirety and taking time to appreciate the diversity and richness of it opens our eyes to many things we've taken for granted. The present moment, for example, is always alive and filled with infinite treasures. It contains far more than we are capable of receiving. See the clouds, the trees, the birds, children playing, the colors all around. The flower blooms, the insect hums, the ant crawls, night follows day—see the moon and stars. There is more beauty and joy in each day than we can ever fully appreciate.

Yet we continue to live our lives focused on future destinations—when the mortgage is paid; when my obligations are fulfilled; when I'm rich; when I meet that special someone; when things are different. Yes, all that will be fine, but what about today? What about this very moment?

There is a Zen practice called "drinking deeply" that involves breaking through the restrictions of a busy mind to fully appreciate everything for what it is. When you're eating, you experience eating fully—the taste, the color, the texture of the food. When you're in the garden, everything becomes special: the flowers, the sky, the air, the hum of the insects, the feel of the earth below your feet. Nothing else is needed. Everything just is. And you are there, noticing and appreciating. It takes practice but we too can learn to do this in our own way, with our families, at our job, in our busy life. We can take the time to do it.

Sometimes one needs to turn everything upside down to make sense of it. What if feeling the wind on your face, hugging your child, laughing with a friend, taking the family out on a picnic, helping someone in need, watching the sunset, carrying out the garbage, going for walks, having friends over for dinner . . . what if this is what it's all about? What if this is what's really important? It's something to stop and consider as we race through our daily lives.

Let us also see the beauty that exists in one another's hearts. Too often we forget this. It is good to remind ourselves that there is much goodness in the world, in the human heart. You will not see it on TV. You will not read about it in the newspapers. But it is there for all to see. Let us acknowledge the fact that for every assault, murder, fraud we hear about, a thousand acts of kindness are performed by ordinary people. We do in fact live in a world where people constantly help one another.

You don't believe that? You do not see it? Put down your newspaper. Turn off your TV. Come take a walk in your own neighborhood. Open your eyes. Feel people's hearts. There is beauty here. Goodness, generosity, love, concern, fellowship everywhere. See the woman who teaches English to the new immigrant. Another who visits the hospital to bring flowers and companionship to a fellow worker. Still another who bakes a cake to take to her elderly aunt. And another again who comforts a friend in a time of sorrow. See the man who coaches little league and buys his players a coke and burger after the game with money from his own pocket. Another who fixes a friend's car for no remuneration. Still another who organizes a community event. And another working in a soup kitchen to feed the homeless. Are you surprised? Did you not know that the world is a beautiful place to live? Did you not know that people's hearts are good? Look in your own heart—is it not good? There are countless others too. Do not be deceived.

Andy Warhol said that life is art, and he was more right than he knew. Each of us is an artist and our life is our canvas. It is ours to create with whatever colors and images we choose. No one can or will paint it for us. No one can live our life but us, and we create according to our courage, vision and understanding.

Every person's life is unique. And the greatest masterpiece one can ever create is that of a life well lived.

Have fun, be successful, make lots of money, be someone who makes a difference, and above all else, don't forget the view.

Visit with John at Home

As a writer committed to staying in touch with his readers, John Kehoe personally invites you to join him via the Internet to share your Mind Power questions and observations. Each month, from his home, John will respond to a selection of correspondence on matters of interest to his ever-expanding community of readers and students. You'll also find this exciting new site loaded with important news and information updates, tour schedules, interesting links, and tips on using Mind Power to get the most out of life! Contact John by directing your browser to:

http://www.learnmindpower.com

Other books by John Kehoe

Mind Power Into the 21st Century
A Vision of Power and Glory
The Practice of Happiness